Love to

CW00540176

Smiley and Me

By Asher Senator

Smiley and Me

By Asher Senator

Voice In The Open Wilderness

3

Asher Senator – Author

First published in Great Britain in 2014 by VOICE IN THE OPEN WILDERNESS PUBLISHING COMPANY.

ISBN 978-0-9935110-0-4

A catalogue record for this book is available from the British Library

Printed in Great Britain by Catford Print, London

Voice In The Open Wilderness
www.vitowmedia.com
110 Union Road
Clapham
London SW8 2SH

This is dedicated to all fans, not just of Smiley Culture, but also of UK Reggae MCs in general. Along with my tribute to Smiley Culture, it is also my utmost intention to give a full, transparent and genuine account of the time when UK Reggae MCs were the talk of England and the world.

CONTENTS

PART TWO

Author's Introduction

Greetings and love with the blessing of the greatest of all Creators – Creator of Heaven and Earth and the Universe and all therein, Controller of sources external and within, and Co-ordinator of all life herein.

I greet you in my original music name of Asher Senator and welcome you to a cultured and exciting account of a friendship that lasted over decades between Smiley Culture and me. Before I extend and reveal my perception of what I consider to be an emotional, heartfelt and passionate journey, I would like to humbly introduce myself – the author. I'm not a professional novelist or biographer, but I've written and performed lyrics throughout my career. It's just that now I'm receiving as much pleasure transferring my thoughts into this format as I did when rhyming words to a killer beat.

My birth name is Peter St. Aubyn – my dad called me Peter after his old boss back in Guyana, and St. Aubyn comes from his side of the family. The name Asher Senator was the name afforded me through various deliberations with close friends, including Smiley.

Author's Introduction

I was born in Georgetown, Guyana in 1960 and celebrated my 3rd birthday on board the ship that brought us to England in 1963 (that's right, I came by ship and had to go through the old 'banana boat' mocking about how we got here). Anyhow, my mum and I docked in Southampton on a cold December day and were greeted by my dad, who had left Guyana a year earlier. He'd come to England for work and had already found some in the form of London Transport. He had rented a place in Clapham and sent for my mum and me, for what reason I have no idea, but here we were anyway.

We lived in Clapham up until I reached the age of around twelve when a move was forced upon my mum, my little sister and I, as my mum and dad separated. We lived in Paddington in a bed & breakfast and I remember having to drop my sister to primary school in Clapham and then heading to my secondary school in Stockwell. The additional journey meant I would always be late for school and eventually I had to explain to the head teachers why. They were very understanding and granted me an extra half hour's grace in the mornings. Eventually my mum, my sister and I moved to Lansdowne Green Estate in Stockwell.

Author's Introduction

It was there that I became infatuated with music, and captivated by all the activities that surrounded it - sound systems, having to build speaker boxes, carrying heavyweight equipment to the dances, the stage shows, clashes, fans, enemies and the girls... I loved the whole scene. From primary school to early secondary school, I was credited with being a very good footballer but once the music got me that was it, I had to be a part of it in one way or another. The majority of my family liked soul music and always teased me for liking roots reggae. The first album I ever bought was Burning Spear's 'Man In The Hills'. It's a classic album but when my mum saw it, she began saying that I'm not right in the head. She just couldn't come to terms with me taking my little bit of money and buying a true to the core Rasta album.

Being part of a sound system was my first real engagement with music and I realise now that it was the equivalent of a school and college course all rolled into one. To say that our sound system Buchanan was my real inspiration in the mid '70s would be an understatement. Look, I had sleepless nights over it, I got cuts and bruises carrying it, I stole for it, I was arrested for it, I fought for it, I robbed for it and did whatever else for it.

Author's Introduction

When I was fourteen I used to set my alarm clock in my bedroom for 1 am, sneak out to attend our Buchanan raves and then return home around six in the morning. Not even the beatings from my mum or my dad (who was now kind of coming back around) could quell my desire to be at Buchanan raves. My passion for music followed me throughout my teenage years and soon I was performing on the microphone, and then eventually writing my own original lyrics.

Buchanan sound-system became my surrogate father – it was my apprenticeship, role model and church. It was back then, hoisting cupboard-sized speaker boxes and wiring endless miles of electrical leads that I grew from boy to man. The Buchanan era lasted at least six years, until I started to chat my lyrics on various other sound systems. My first professional music encounter was in the 80s, when after considerable success on the national sound system circuit, I signed as a recording and performing artist to a popular record label of the time called Fashion Records, who already had successful reggae MCs like Laurel and Hardy on their books. I stayed with Fashion Records for two years, recording exclusively with them.

Author's Introduction

I had hits on the UK reggae singles chart with 'Abbreviation Qualification' b/w 'Fast Style Origination' and 'The Big Match'. My album 'JA to UK Clash' alongside the Jamaican DJ Johnny Ringo went to No. 1 in the UK reggae album chart and my solo album for Fashion Records 'Born to Chat,' also climbed into the Top 5. When my sparring partner Smiley Culture and friend Maxi Priest broke into the UK national charts with their hits 'Police Officer' and 'Strolling On', this gave me the opportunity to experience and understand more about the music industry as I witnessed them give TV, radio and live performances all over England. In the '90s a song that I recorded in Brescia, Italy called 'Move It Up' went to No. 1 in the Italian and other European dance charts. Its success enabled me to tour more widely around Europe and in countries where I often felt like the only African descendant around. These experiences gave me confidence, and then a number of other British artists approached me to see if they could get involved once my videos were shown on The Box and MTV. The array of talent back in the UK was nothing new to me but I now had more knowledge of the business, plus a sense of purpose and some money.

Author's Introduction

I took my earnings from Europe and invested it in studio equipment, and this meant that I could help some of the talent on my doorstep. Initially, I worked with artists from my own age group because I could relate to them and the obstacles they faced in the music business. Soon youngsters and even their parents approached us, hoping we could give them support and I found myself at the helm of a growing movement – one that began as a performance group before it evolved into an organisation and then finally a charity by the name of Code 7, whose objective is to provide in-demand multimedia and mentoring services for disenfranchised young people. I am the CEO of Code 7 and it is my duty to manage general operations and in particular raise funds. To think that back in the '80s and even the early '90s all I wanted to do was write lyrics and more lyrics! Now my lyrical skills are being utilised writing plans, reports and funding applications. To help me manage this charity, I made sure to gain qualifications in Teacher Training 7407, Leadership and Management, ICT and even Conflict Resolution. In order to maintain our success we constantly carry out in-depth studies, researches, evaluations and surveys but the greatest attribute I have is the experience I gained from growing up within the Lambeth community.

Author's Introduction

When I write, I write with the energy that I have received throughout my life – an energy I identify as being bigger than myself.

People kept asking me if I would write a book about my friendship with Smiley Culture and I said no, because I knew that some of the things I had to say would cause controversy. Then after careful consideration I thought to myself, 'CHA, I'M GETTING OLD. THE SMILEY AND ASHER STORY'S COLD – AND SO IT HAS TO BE TOLD.'

Thicker Than Water

Let me give you a brief description of my friend Smiley Culture – namely a six foot, light-skinned, slim black male from London who grabbed life by its horns and rode it at speeds most people could only dream of. His most amazing feat was to become a No. 1 reggae artist after starting from a position of zilch, because it's astonishing to think how he transformed his status from 'broke ass kid without two pennies to rub together' to 'successful production company director of music and African commodities'. Courageous and always the centre of attraction, no matter the occasion or situation. Extravagant but ultimately his bundle of energy helped him in many different ways on the journey to achieve his goal. He showed sentiment favourably, displayed kindness unsparingly and his actions were truly dictated by his emotions.

Anyone attempting to write an account of our friendship would need to have known us extremely well, and understood our minds and way of thinking. They would certainly need to have been a strong inspiration in our lives at crucial and exciting stages. Oh well, I suppose that leaves the writing down to me.

For those of you who know us, I needn't say anymore, but for newcomers to the Smiley Culture and Asher Senator story I can't emphasise how close we were in the early days.

To be specific, Smiley and I were friends since the days of Margaret Thatcher, blues dances and the first Brixton riots. In the early days we were so close that people used to say you don't see one without the other. If by chance we were not together at any time and someone spotted one of us, they would always ask for the other. "Asher, where's Smiley?" or "Smiley, where's Asher?" Some people found it a bit odd that we could be such tight friends, given Smiley's six-foot frame and my lack of height. They'd leap at the opportunity to mock us by calling us names such as the Dynamic Duo. "Look, it's Batman and Robin..."

Smiley and I knew each other so well that we knew which buttons not to press if we didn't want to upset each other. We developed speaking codes that only we could understand, impersonated our favourite music stars and wrote so many lyrics together. We knew what each other liked and disliked, loved and hated and what each other wanted and never wanted.

We liked the same food and drink, and sounded so much alike on the phone that people would be confused about who they were speaking to. We linked up from early in the mornings and then rolled together throughout the days, evenings and nights... Sometimes we'd get home the next day at the same time we'd left the previous morning. We went everywhere together and sometimes laughed so much, we felt as if we were going to die if we didn't stop. We knew the same people because we were always together and although we hadn't gone to the same school, we knew each other's school friends. Our families were linked through us and we ate at each other's homes regularly. We fought wars together against local bad boys and always covered for each other in dire situations. We'd steal cars, drive them for the night and put them back. We camped (waited) for some bad boys who were bothering us to catch them unaware and at one stage in our lives we had to carry weapons so we could defend our lives everywhere we went. I learnt so much from him that it wasn't until looking back that I realised how calculated, creative and intelligent Smiley Culture really was. No task was too much for him since he'd always find a way around tricky situations somehow, as he strived to make money.

By way of contrast I was more laid back and quite content to let things happen through steady perseverance. I was writing lyrics and wanted to gain success with music just like Culture did with his hit single 'Police Officer'. Culture got through and gave his all to his music career but it always seemed that unless he achieved a million-zillion seller, he would always be exploring different avenues to make the kind of money he desired and as he used to say, deserved.

When Smiley started to make money through his music career, he immediately started to help people. If he bought a car, he'd ensure that I got the equivalent. He bought home stereos for a few girls and fed people daily. Some people didn't understand him and used to say they didn't like him but Culture didn't care. He was articulate, and someone who didn't like him today could easily be honouring him tomorrow. He cared about who and what he cared about and that was it. Anything else had no relevance to his life. He knew the psychology of people and knew that money talks and bullshit walks. Most of his time was spent thinking about his next few moves. He loved movies and studied African history intensely.

Sometimes he'd phone me and say to come over and watch a film or documentary and believe me, every time I went to watch something he'd recommended I would always be motivated by it.

PART ONE

Miss Coarsey

She may not have been every man's dream but Miss Coarsey was certainly a queen in the eyes of us Buchanan boys. She may have proved a nightmare to some of us but at the end of the day we all appreciated her and gave her maximum respect – so much so that even the girls who used to hang round the sound accepted the significance of her existence. All the residents in the area knew of her and looked at her as they passed by, wondering how she survived the nightly escapades she endured. Sometimes Smiley and I would check up on her in the middle of the night just to make sure that she was okay. We'd chill by her side and speak excitedly about the adventures that we'd experienced with her. Most times it didn't take long before other members of the sound would join us, and then the reasoning could last hours.

Miss Coarsey was our chariot, our royal carriage and queen of the ghetto. She was bearer of our tribulations and the keeper of many secrets – a resting-place for many a weary head, and a symbol of our commitment to Buchanan. Miss Coarsey was the home and transporter of our sound system.

Miss Coarsey

Yes, our beloved old truck that earned the name Miss Coarsey simply because she was coarse looking, coarse sounding and needed to be handled rough. As noisy as a tank and equally as slow she had anaemic looking, faded green bodywork, fully bald tyres, no handbrake, weak foot brakes, dodgy suspension, rusty bodywork, a stiff clutch, vision blurring windscreen wipers and on top of everything she needed a push start *ALL OF THE TIME*. Hey, I'm serious. It took maybe six or more people to push start Miss Coarsey, and they'd have to put in great effort to have the slightest hope of starting her. I was the designated driver and must have been around sixteen at the time so to me it was exciting, exhilarating and a rush. Smiley admired my commitment and used to tell everyone that I was the driver of our truck. Junior, Buchanan's founder, and Ron 'The Builder', our amplifier technician, were the only other people spirited enough to take the wheel of this high-risk vehicle. Buchanan was a decent sized sound system. We owned around twelve sets of speaker boxes that were all nearly wardrobe size; a record box that was so heavy no individual could lift it and several other weighty pieces of equipment like valve amplifiers.

Miss Coarsey

Miss Coarsey also had to cope with the scores of people who rode in her. Given the loads she had to carry; her inadequacies and how often we used her, it was incredible that she always delivered, because despite her high maintenance, and all the labour and attention that she commanded, Miss Coarsey got us to every single dance we ever played at. I remember one memorable, but embarrassing night when we were due to play in Crystal Palace, and Miss Coarsey refused to climb one of the hills on the journey there. We had to stop midway up the hill, flag the traffic past us and let her roll back down. We then found an alternative route that was less steep, and eventually arrived at the dance in one piece. Another time after a dance, I was driving Miss Coarsey at around six in the morning and coming off Loughborough Road to turn right onto Brixton Road when I decided to beat the traffic lights before they changed to red. As she turned, loaded with equipment and people, she struggled badly and her right side lifted off the ground. It seemed like an eternity as we all sat waiting in deafening silence as she hung in the air, defying gravity. Everything was happening in slow motion and then BOOM!! Miss Coarsey's right wheels hit the ground again to relieved cheers all round.

Miss Coarsey

The people in the back cheered so loud that we could hear them amidst all the wild applause and constant engine noise happening in the front cabin. Somehow, Miss Coarsey trudged along, carrying us and our equipment to dance after dance, and the remarkable thing was that she always made it home. One time Buchanan were about to play a dance in Wolverhampton when Gary Mason pulled up to greet Smiley and I on Wandsworth Road in a Wolseley – a car known as "the black man's Rolls Royce" back in the 1970s, we saw it as the perfect way for us to travel in comfort. When we questioned him as to where he'd got it, his reasoning that he'd "bought it in a car auction" was good enough for us so we filled up the tank and sped away on the M1 like boy racers, leaving Ron, who was driving Miss Coarsey, in our rear view. We laughed out loud as we burned tyres, and saw Miss Coarsey drifting further and further into the distance. The fun continued throughout the night as we teased and taunted the others who'd all travelled in Miss Coarsey. We teased them about how cold, rough and noisy their journey must have been and how much worse it was going to be on the way back in the morning. Putting more petrol in the Wolseley, we shot down the motorway without a care for those we'd left behind.

Miss Coarsey

Everything was fine as we headed home doing approximately 110 mph, but then disaster struck. Smoke started to emerge from our engine and the panic started. The fact that we were only half way down the M1 made the situation really dire. We yelled and as the smoke thickened we yelled more. Eventually we had no option but to pull over on the hard shoulder and as Gary started shouting, "It's gonna blow, It's gonna blow!" we grabbed our jackets and ran as far from the car as possible. Thick white smoke engulfed the car and began to drift across the motorway. There was no way we were going back to that vehicle. We knew motorway assistance would deal with the car but for us, there was only one way left for us to get home – Miss Coarsey. It was ages before we spotted her big chunky shape coming towards us in the distance. We had to run onto the motorway to ensure that Ron saw us flagging him down. There was never a time that Smiley and I were happier to see Miss Coarsey. We jumped in the back with the others and the equipment and were so grateful that night for her familiar coldness, roughness and noisiness. Every journey in Miss Coarsey took longer than necessary and we could feel the full effects of her infirmities from the back of the truck.

Miss Coarsey

I tried to sleep but found it impossible as she swayed from side to side, bobbled up and down and roared every so often. I brought Smiley's attention to Gary, who'd somehow managed to fall asleep. His head bounced up and down on a wooden framed speaker box as he slept soundly while snoring nearly as loud as Miss Coarsey's roar. Smiley and I watched in amazement as Gary slept all the way back to London. I imagine it was those same early qualities Gary possessed that eventually helped him to become the British heavyweight boxing champion at one stage in his life. Miss Coarsey had got us home but Gary never recovered the car from the motorway, which made us slightly suspicious of how he'd attained it in the first place. Anyhow, Miss Coarsey was our saviour. She was the one that we praised on many occasions. So many people respected Miss Coarsey and referred to her by name. Anyone who had any affiliation with Buchanan would have certainly travelled in her at some point and anyone who travelled in her probably had to help push start her. She loved catching people out after a long night of raving. All dressed up, looking prim and proper and feeling the effects from their raving exploits, hitch-hikers would end up soiled, exasperated and short of breath after pushing Miss Coarsey a few times.

Miss Coarsey

Buchanan's following was healthy to say the least. Every young person in the area grew to be a part of the sound in one way or another, and so she was spoilt for choice when it came to her customary push. We loved Miss Coarsey. Tears filled my eyes and my heart hurt badly when she was burnt down, murdered like a gangster. The news travelled quickly and I was unfortunate to witness the last stages of her existence. It was too late to save her as she had saved us on so many occasions. She crumbled under the flames and I could hear crackling and popping as our equipment burned inside her. Had it been the work of guys from a rival sound system, it might have been a little more bearable as we would have surely retaliated. Had it been members of the National Front it may have been a little more tolerable, because that probably would have sparked a massive riot. Even if it had been the police it would have been somewhat more understandable, as we already knew they didn't like the loud and beautiful reggae noise we made.

No, it was none of the above. Miss Coarsey was burnt down by a girl – a girl that had a grievance with Buchanan's founder Junior, and who had chilled, hung out and raved with Buchanan for years.

It was a girl that had fought and stolen for the sound, and someone I regarded as one of the last people who would have done anything to hurt Buchanan. That incident spelt the end of an era and even though Buchanan sound-system was rebuilt, it was never the same without Miss Coarsey.

Chapter 1

The Young Smiley Culture

One Saturday afternoon in the mid-1970s, I was at home and listening to some reggae music on my little stereo, which barely worked. At this time in my life, I lived with my dad on South Lambeth Road in Stockwell, in a little flat located on the first floor of a small council block that, apart from my dad and I, was occupied by elderly white residents. The block only had two floors and so when I say "small block," I mean it had around twelve flats in total. The residents were lovely people and I don't remember any of them ever complaining about me, or my music. It was my dad who was the worry for me. He hated it when I played music loud, so I'd wait until he left to go to work and then blaze my music so loud that anyone would think there was a rave going on!

On more than one occasion my dad stormed into the flat while I was pumping some heavy beats and yelled up the stairs at the top of his voice, "IT'S TOO FUCKING LOUD!"

I always tried to time it right when it came to playing my music, but when those beats took me I would lose all track of time and regularly end up on the receiving end of my dad's wrath.

The Young Smiley Culture

The reason I happened to be living with dad was because I couldn't bear mum nagging about me finding a job anymore, and so now it was dad's turn to find out what she'd been complaining about for so long. He was so happy when I'd first asked to move in with him, because he'd probably thought that he was getting one over on mum, and anytime he could rub her face in it, then believe me he did. Anyhow, he was rapidly learning about how the average teenager growing up in 1970s' Britain tackled obstacles in their life - by pushing up that dial on the stereo and escaping into a dense bass-line. He didn't like it one bit and I knew it was only a matter of time before he too, would want to be rid of me.

One particular afternoon I was pumping that music with an overwhelming passion. The unfortunate events that had happened the night before at a Buchanan rave held firm in my mind and I was trying to extinguish the memories by playing positive and uplifting music. I could still picture the people who were hurt during the massive fight that had kicked off between warring sound-system members inside and outside a club in Battersea.

Punches and kicks exploded all around as perfectly aimed bottles flew through the air, spitting out their alcoholic residue before detonating on an unfortunate target. Speaker boxes got boxed, turntables were overturned and amplifiers got amputated. The wreckage in the club resembled a news report from the Vietnam War. Whoever said that, "when music hits you feel no pain" had clearly never witnessed a South London sound clash. All night I kept thinking, 'Why do we have to fight all the time? Why can't we just go out, jam to the music and have a good time sometimes?'

Such thoughts continued to eat away at me all night and into the next afternoon. I blazed out one of my favourite tracks by Dennis Brown and deejay Big Youth.

"Running up and down won't help in this time. We all got to be positive in our minds..." There I was, singing along totally lost in the music and it suddenly dawned on me that I knew the words to the whole song, including Big Youth's lyrics. I even thought that I sounded a bit like Big Youth, whilst pondering how I could put my theory to the test. I realised that the only way to capture my voice would be through a tape recording.

The Young Smiley Culture

I had a cassette tape player that had a built-in microphone and so I found an old TDK cassette tape and eagerly put it in.

I recorded a few takes until I was satisfied that I'd done a good enough job and then I listened back to them. To my surprise, I was taken aback by what I heard. The recording sounded quite good and yes, I thought that I sounded somewhat like Big Youth, but I needed more confirmation. As quickly as I could, I got myself ready and made my way towards Lansdowne Green Estate where Smiley lived, because I needed him to hear it. He and I had first met each other a few years previously, when Buchanan played at a house dance in Union Grove.

I was reasoning with a few of the sound crew in the passageway when this smartly dressed, light-skinned young man joined in the banter. I'd already caught a glimpse of him observing us earlier, and remember wondering who he was and where he was from. It wasn't long before he began laughing with us as if he'd been a part of the clique from day dot, and eventually he spun a few wise cracks of his own.

He introduced himself as Smiley, and quickly demonstrated the characteristics that exemplified his confidence and ability to communicate with others.

I liked his energy right away and when he told me that I had a funny personality, our friendship materialised from there on.

We started to link up in Lansdowne Green Estate and soon became regular sparring partners. Our friendship was at an early stage but Smiley gave that no thought when asking me about a girl that I was supposedly dating.

He wanted to know if I liked her because he really wanted to 'move to her'. It's a "mano-a-mano" thing, and I would have done the same. I wasn't exactly love-struck for this girl and so when I gave him the all clear he didn't hesitate to sweep her off her feet. Unfortunately, this girl never got over it. She developed a reserved hatred towards me that was evident from the screw-faced expression she displayed every time our paths met. It was as "if looks could kill, blood in your eyes" type of scenario but it's nothing, and I lived with it.

Smiley was overwhelmed by the excitement of the sound system and what we represented. He became a convert and soon immersed himself in the life of Buchanan. In his own words, it was a blessing to be able to come over to Junior's flat during the day so he could join with us in developing the sound.

He would stick around after we'd finished working on it and Smiley, myself and a few others found ourselves spending more and more time together.

Eventually, "more and more" became every day for Smiley and myself, and also anyone else who was close to us and could keep up. Once we'd become friends, we used to hang out together around the sound system, either somewhere locally or at one of our homes. We loved music, and were so enthusiastic about Buchanan that we happily helped to build speaker boxes and carry them whenever we played out. We'd hoist these speaker boxes into tiny elevators that smelled of piss, and manoeuvre them up and down council estate staircases throughout the darkest of winters, and sweltering hot summers. With all the banter and jokes going around, we couldn't have been happier. In dances back then, the only real thing you would say on the microphone was "Man a who say...?" It was a known dancehall chant, and guaranteed to get the crowd shouting for a rewind of the track that was playing.

By learning one of our hero's lyrics and chanting it back I'd taken it a step further, although I thought it was just a little passing inspiration, and would soon die out...

Until I played the tape to Smiley, that is. I arrived at the front of his block of flats and prepared to make my way up to the fourth floor where he lived. I'd grown up in Lansdowne Green Estate, and so I was absolutely used to the surroundings.

This estate held many a story and secrets for us. It was a large estate and obviously housed hundreds of people. It served up all sorts of "life" recipes for us, whether hiding us when we were running from the police, or acting as a maze for girls to give us the run around when we were after them for some nookie. It was the place where I'd spent most of my teenage years and so although I didn't live there anymore, it was still my home estate.

I was so eager to play the tape to Smiley that I couldn't wait for the lift. I sprinted up the concrete staircase and reached the fourth floor panting heavily, like when a lion pauses to catch its breath before the final kill. I recovered my composure at Smiley's front door and then knocked. The door opened and his girlfriend of the time let me in. When I entered Smiley's room, he was laying on the bed. His bedroom only had enough room for one chair and I claimed that, so his girlfriend sat on the bed next to him.

Smiley liked to wear stylish clothes and that was how he was dressed, in a stylish beige coloured dressing gown. There was a pair of slippers beside his bed that looked as if they had been kicked off and been left exactly how they landed. The plush velvet wallpaper contained hints of the same dark blue found in the thick carpet and his bed sheets, pillowcases and accessories were all shades of blue as well, as were the ornaments and fittings. The cream coloured curtains hanging at the windows were the only decorative features that weren't blue in fact.

His bed was low to the ground, which was excellent because it was the perfect height for me to relax my feet on the bed frame whenever I was sat in the chair beside it. Smiley never once objected to me dangling and resting my feet right beside him on his bedside. It was a standard requirement to take your shoes off at the front door so I always made sure that my feet were not too smelly as I'm sure Smiley would have certainly objected to my feet being so close to his nose! He was already making enough money to possess some of the finer things in life – items of equipment like his TV, video and stereo system that most of us found hard to come by.

He had a Marantz stereo system, which was a reputable Japanese brand in those days. Its' operative heart was situated on top of a small glass fronted cabinet, and there were speakers placed in all four corners of the room. I couldn't wait to hear the tape on this stereo system and so as I sat down I said immediately "you've got to listen to this tape!" Getting up, he took it out of my hand and made his way over to the system. When he asked me what was on the tape I simply replied "Me!" He laughed and while putting in the tape he couldn't resist asking, "Wha', you turn singer, rude bwoy?"

He pressed the play button on the system. The first sound we heard was the hiss coming from my overused tape cassette, and then after a few seconds my voice kicked in. It didn't bother me, playing my recording to Smiley but I was apprehensive and felt somewhat awkward at his girlfriend being there. I could handle Smiley telling me that it was rubbish if he thought so, but the thought of him saying that in front of his girlfriend wasn't on. As they listened to the tape, I watched Smiley and his girlfriend's reactions closely, my head turning from side to side like a spectator at Wimbledon's Centre Court.

Suddenly Smiley jumped up in excitement and yelled, "You sound just like them Dread!" Phew - they liked it! I combed my hands through my dreadlocked hair. He and his girlfriend had approved of my recording and it was thumbs up, all round.

Smiley was certainly inspired to give it a go himself and he too, tried unlocking his hidden talent. We started to learn lyrics by our favourite artists and Smiley bought a good quality microphone so that we could sound even better. We were in his flat rehearsing every day, although we didn't anticipate this DJ thing would actually amount to anything. It was just a "love for it" thing that we had. We copied those Jamaican lyrics to a "T," and had fun chatting them on Buchanan sound-system in the dances. As we became recognised for our abilities on the microphone, friends and other people started to bring whistles to the dances. Some people's lungs were incredible since they blew those whistles constantly by way of encouragement, even though we were "pirating" lyrics.

It was only after the track 'Hard Times' by Pablo Gad came out that we were eventually forced to start writing original lyrics. Smiley and I had learnt that song well, and were going to perform the lyrics on this particular night at a Buchanan dance.

We geared ourselves up and arrived at the dance ready to make it our big night, only to hear someone else performing the same lyrics. We were gutted, but said that we'd still perform it. Later that night, just as we were about to step up and perform the song, another man beat us to the mic. He too sang the lyrics from the song 'Hard Times.' This experience taught us that the only way we could become respected DJs was to write our own lyrics and there you have it - Smiley and Asher were to become writers and "chatters" of original lyrics. "Chatters" – that was the term back then for DJs who performed their lyrics live. Everyone used the terminology "chatter" whether they were DJs or not. We would hear people saying things like, "There's them chatters from Buchanan" or "Chat a lyrics for me, rude boy". Smiley wrote clever and witty lyrics from the start, and that accurately represented his character and personality. He was already making money on the road through his hustling abilities; hence one of his lyrics entitled 'Money Move, Mek Some Money'. He explained that a few years before we'd met, he'd spent time in a detention centre for burglary, so his jailhouse lyric 'Life in a Prison No Sweet' was written from real life experience. He hadn't liked being locked up one bit, and this had motivated him to pursue a more legal hustle.

He would often state that he could never ever take a custodial sentence again. When his girlfriend became his baby mother, Smiley used to collect her child benefit book, cash the money and buy things like watches, ornaments and other saleable items that he could hustle to people on the road. He started to turn over a nice little change and at one stage he would carry up to a thousand pounds on him every day. He'd show a local youth called Freddie his wad of money and I remember Freddie saying to him, "that's the same money you're walking with all the time man!" Smiley slept, ate and dreamt money until sometimes it would bug me that he was actually speaking about money again. I would ask him if he would never stop talking about money, money, money and he used to reply, "Dread, we need to make big money because the people who run this world have no pity!" Sometimes it was just about having fun but to be honest, Smiley had an entrepreneurial spirit and was relentless in his pursuit of wealth. He was driven by the fear of losing his freedom, and the desire to escape the lack of, and need for money. Money therefore have fi' run under Jah Jah moon, stars and sun but Smiley also had a deeply cultural side to him, and which certainly warranted him having the name "Culture" as his DJ surname.

When we sat down to find a DJ surname for him and the name Culture was thrown into the hat, everyone who was present agreed that it sounded good, and worked well. "Smiley Culture" suited him as he studied African history intensely, and loved movies with meaning, that were based on real life. Still his preference of movies was extensive as he introduced me to movies such as Scarface, The Exorcist, Dog Day Afternoon and the first IRA movie I ever saw The Long Good Friday with Bob Hoskins. He also knew of all the great African-American leaders and would focus a lot of his lyrics on their ideals. He wrote lyrics inspired by stories out of the Bible such as 'Solomon Was A Very Wise Man' and 'It Was Written In Genesis,' and was courageous in promoting African and Caribbean culture. Smiley loved to be the centre of attraction no matter the occasion or situation, but his spirit was as cultural as anyone I have ever met. Some said he was extravagant but he was a sentimental person who displayed kindness unsparingly, and whose actions were often dictated by his emotions.

However, Smiley had a thing about cars and was ecstatic when I phoned him one day and said, 'Smiley, I've got a car'.

Although we'd both driven many different cars, neither of us had ever owned our own. Smiley told me that he was an expert driver who'd passed his test at a very early age, and had even driven a car to school. In those days we had a bunch of keys that fitted a variety of cars and so we'd take someone's car at night, go raving and put it back in the morning without them ever noticing, although they must have wondered why their petrol kept going down.

Anyhow it was Miss Maud, my son's grandmother who asked me in a Jamaican accent, "Peter, you can drive? You want a car?" and then gave me a reddish orange Hillman Avenger that had been left by a man who'd died while renting a room in her house. The car only needed new tyres, brakes and an exhaust pipe, which I looked forward to sorting out when I finally raised the cash. Still, I was so excited that all I had done was pump up the tyres when I rang Smiley. He was as excited as me, if not more so and said, "Pick me up dread". This car had no MOT, no tax or insurance and the tyres were bald but I picked him up and we went out driving. Wow, is that how we rolled those days? It was SHOW OFF TIME – "WE'VE GOT A CAR!" – and we wanted everyone to see.

We picked up a bunch of friends until the car was full, drove to Brixton and were rattling down Ferndale Road when a car driven by an elderly black man cut in front of us. I realise now that no way was my car going to stop in an emergency. Me driving, Smiley in the passenger seat, the back full of youths, bad brakes and bald tyres... A collision was inevitable and SMASH! We went into the side of the man's car.

This man was definitely in the wrong because he'd been indicating to turn right, we went to pass on the left and he suddenly turned back to the left. I said to the driver, who was Jamaican, "You know you were in the wrong!" and he said "No way, I have been driving in this country for twenty years and I have never..." and so on. I told him his indicator was still indicating the other way but he just went to the car, turned it off and said "Nah, man..." By this time, all the friends who'd been packed in the back of my car said they had things to do and went off, leaving Smiley and I to deal with it.

The other driver and I exchanged details and Smiley and I pulled out the dented wing so we were able to drive again. Boy, did we cuss after that, saying how those guys weren't real friends because of the way they'd just left us.

It let us know that we had to stay tight because the way things stood, we didn't have too many friends who genuinely cared about us out there. That day was the catalyst for our friendship to become tighter than the bond between Batman and Robin, Abbot and Castello or even Starsky and Hutch.

Smiley wasn't perfect, and he had a nasty temper that would surface from time to time. He was always controlled with me but with his girlfriends, the police or strangers who pissed him off, he wasn't a nice guy. I wasn't too far behind with my belligerent behaviour towards my woman and others but I eventually managed to control my hostile streak and ranted and raved more instead. When I conquered my wayward behaviour, Smiley used to say that he was dealing with things more calmly just like me. Oh well... At least he was conscious about it and spoke about changing his ways with genuine sincerity. On many occasions I'd have to try and cool Smiley down from either fighting with his girlfriend or having it out with someone on the road. Sometimes even I was wary of his outbursts but for some reason he listened to me more than anyone else. He and I had our differences but we still built up a trust that lasted throughout our lives.

When we saw some local youths on the road displaying their madness and careless behaviour we decided to have talk codes that would let the other know if we were ever in trouble. For instance, if he rang me and said, "bring the oldest records we've got", I knew it was time to round up some troops because trouble's about to happen.

As time progressed, Smiley started to buy his own cars. A Datsun Cherry, a Fiat and a Lancia were his first real cars. Sometimes he used to drive very fast but his confidence always made me feel safe. We never really had much going on outside of our area so we mainly drove up, down and around locally anyway. One summer day Smiley was in his orange Audi, speeding along a side road next to Lansdowne Green Estate with me beside him in the passenger seat. All of a sudden, from between parked cars, a young black girl burst into the road in front of us. I've heard people reflect on moments like these by saying it was like watching in slow motion, but this incident happened in a flash. It was too late to stop and we hit her hard. The poor girl went flying but in her panic got back up and while screaming in a high pitched voice, ran across the road to her mother who was shaking in total shock.

The girl collapsed again on the other side of the pavement. Smiley and I were shook up and he immediately said to me, "You've got a license dread and I don't, so please say you were driving". With that, we exchanged seats quickly and no one seemed to notice. By the time we came out of the car, the girl's father was running down the road with a knife in his hand and fuming. He was shouting in a Jamaican accent, "I gwan kill one of dem driver yah, dem keep driving down this road too fast".

As far as this father was concerned I was the driver and he rushed towards me menacingly. He grabbed me by the collar and put his knife to my throat. I was terrified but then I heard the girl's mother saying, "No, no it wasn't his fault, she just ran in front of the car". The man reluctantly let me go and started crying uncontrollably. Smiley and I went to the hospital straight away and we were upset to find out that she had a broken leg and cuts, but at the same time relieved that she was not fatally injured. The parents didn't press charges and we made sure we kept in contact with the girl for a long time after. Even when we began to do shows and arrived back to the estate, we would always look for this girl and give her money.

She used to love us and maybe she told this story to her friends after we became famous although if she reads this, it's only now that she'll discover it was Smiley who knocked her down and not me, sorry.

Smiley started to buy music and this enabled us to keep up-to-date with our lyrics while we were there in his mum's flat, writing and chatting lyrics for most of the day and night. Vico D and Willie Major were our closest friends, and both of them would practice and rehearse lyrics with us. Vico was a humble character who would not take any shit from anyone and as for Major, I can only describe him as a loose cannon. Vico had a style that merged singing and chanting while Willie Major was making steady progress with his lyrics as a DJ although we had to be extra careful around him, as he tended to get into quite a few mix ups that he found hard to get out of. He even went as far as asking police why they'd stopped him after he'd grazed their car with a stolen car that he was driving while under the influence of alcohol. He was truly something else. Still, he and Vico were always fun to be around and they gave Smiley and I plenty of jokes.

Every night, when Vico and Willie left Smiley's to go home after raiding his fridge and smoking up all of his stash of Brixton's finest, they'd whistle up from the ground floor and when Smiley looked out of the window they'd shout, "We used you again, you f-o-o-l..." It was truly funny and Smiley used to just laugh and accept it as being tongue in cheek. All of us loved going to the famous Brixton front line on Railton Road where you were guaranteed entertainment no matter the time or the people involved. To be totally honest, we learned some means of survival by just chilling on the sidelines and watching the big men do their thing. Smiley and I would humorously recite things that we'd heard on the front line wherever we went. We used to hang out on the road outside or inside the houses on Railton Road that were used as hustling outlets and gambling points, and just observe the actions of the main people involved. It was a place where egos dominated, and everyone believed they were the top man in Brixton. People's attitudes and values were so different then, because I can recall people's astonishment if a knife was ever used in a fight and on another level, the fear that swept the community whenever a gun was fired. We witnessed petty arguments, minor squabbles and main event street fights.

The Young Smiley Culture

There were wars and rumours of whores but nothing matched Brixton's front line for colour, vibrancy and a sense of life laid bare. Hustlers would have crocus bags of cannabis out in the open on the roadside and next to it would be a pile of bookie's slips they used to serve weed in. Police said and did nothing apart from on the odd occasion when they raided the gambling houses. I am so glad that we never got caught up in any police raids because, in comparison to what was really going down we were innocents, so that would have been totally unfair although some people would say "You make your bed..."

Anyway, as I stated we were out for fun and vibes and Brixton front line was one of the places where we found that. The slangs and road-talk codes were something else and the way no main person allowed another main person to take liberties always gave it an edge. Smiley and I were always picking up on certain things. One day we just were chilling when out of the blue we heard a known bad boy shout out at the top of his voice, "The next person to build a spliff without asking me and then comes to me for weed, I WILL SPIT IN DEM RIZLA..." We saw one weed hustler turn away purchasers because they'd bought weed from a different seller on another occasion.

That was a sin in their eyes and so it was essential to be aware of from whom and how you bought your weed. New punters would have to be careful because the opportunists on the front line who stole, robbed or conned for a living would swoop upon any weakness. Guys would leave their girlfriends in their car while they bought their draw of weed only to return to find someone in their car checking out their woman.

Some guys got back to their cars minus their possessions while some didn't even make it back to their cars at all, since running for their lives was the wiser option.

The vibes of the front line attracted us in such a way that we began to rave at dances held around there. These dances were something else and just going to some as young youths made us feel more grown up, although the risks of getting caught up in some form of problem always lingered. One night when Smiley and I were in a dance on the front line with Vico D, Willie Major and a few other friends, we saw a man standing at the top of the stairs putting something white in his spliff. We pondered amongst ourselves until we decided that someone should go and ask the man what it was. We chose Willy Major, so he went up the stairs and approached the man.

Major asked him what was in his spliff and this resulted in the man snappishly yelling at him. The strange thing was that although this man was yelling, hardly any sound came out of his mouth. We could just about hear him yelling, "WHAT'S IT GOT TO DO WID YOU?"

We eventually found out that the man was taking cocaine and we vowed never to touch it, as we were strictly Ribena and sensimilla people. Nevertheless, we made fun out of the man's statement every time we remembered it and imitated the same hoarse efforts he'd made to yell out, "WHAT'S IT GOT TO DO WID YOU?" Willie Major's crazy side surfaced quite frequently and one night on the front line he took it upon himself to blurt out "Boy, that bredder's ugly!" as a man passed us to go upstairs in the rave. Little did Willie Major know, but the man's friend was behind him and heard everything that had been said. Now the man Major had insulted was a known bad man in Brixton, and broader than three Willie Majors put together. Oh man, this guy was fuming as he came running down the stairs shouting, "ANYONE WHO HAS SOMETHING TO SAY ABOUT ME BETTER SAY IT TO MY FACE..." Obviously, Major didn't speak again.

Smiley and I later told him to watch his mouth and to be careful what he says but it wasn't much of a surprise to us when he decided to play the fool in another hardcore dance filled with Brixton bad boys. It was darker than dark inside the dance, and Major kept turning on the light switch to see if he could spot anyone he knew. It wasn't long before one of the Brixton name brands came over and harshly told Major to stop turning on the light and that if he did it again, there would be serious consequences. Guess what? Yes, Major turned the light switch on again and the guy went crazy. He and the owner of a notorious sound system grabbed Major and pushed him into a side room, so we rushed in to follow.

They roughed him up a little, told him that if he wasn't such a little youth they would hurt him badly and with that they let him go. We were relieved as we didn't have a chance against all those big men and Major clearly got the message because he didn't turn the light on again. Once more, Smiley and I warned Major to watch himself and especially when he was with us, which was most of the time anyway. Despite such incidents, it was a pleasure being out on the front line and hearing and seeing so many things that we regarded as inspirational.

The Young Smiley Culture

We started to incorporate some of the things that we witnessed into our lyrics but we always made sure to stay away from writing and chatting anything that could have incriminated anyone, or jeopardised our standing in Brixton. It was a "mind your mouth" kind of thing. Smiley, Vico, Major and I sparred together for a considerable amount of time until suddenly, out of the blue Vico and Willie told us they were going to do their own thing. Smiley used to say, "anyone who leaves me will flop" and when Vico and Willie later fell on hard times, Smiley pointed to this as evidence. He certainly had a way with mind games and as time went on I knew that I always had to be alert to his scheming and lively personality. He would even go as far as pretending that someone had told him something, to make people admit or talk about things. Soon after Vico and Major left, Militant Mikey and Fox joined the posse, and both remained close with us for many years. Their loyalty was second to none and it was clear that they, like Smiley and I, were even prepared to die for the cause. All I know is that we had a cause, even though we couldn't actually define it. Having said that, Smiley surely had a cause to become rich and made sure that the four of us stayed together as a unit, to help fulfil the mission. Mikey and Fox were true soldiers.

They were ready for anything and everything, no matter the time, place or event. Mikey was quite short, trimly built and full of energy. Girls always talked about his chocolate brown skin and cute baby face. He had a vibrant personality and always wanted to be on the move. Anything that came up he would always say, "Let's do it!" Fox was a more humble character but he always generated a serious aura about him. His slim physique, light brown skin and sharply defined features made him one of the girls' favourites everywhere we went. We started to call him "The Peacemaker," as he made it his duty to jump in the middle of fights to keep the peace, whether he knew the fighters or not.

Mikey and I were physical fitness freaks while Smiley and Fox only committed to occasional fitness training, but could still give anyone a run for their money when it came to physical fitness and strength. Smiley would only do press-ups when he had trapped wind as he used to say they helped to clear it. I can't verify if it really worked or not because I did so many of them. Mikey and I were knocking out around a hundred press-ups at a time, so it was impossible for me to examine Smiley's theory.

The Young Smiley Culture

By way of contrast, he used to do around ten press-ups, call it a day and then move onto something else as far removed from physical exercise as possible, yet he'd still offer to race anyone who looked like they had some money on them. Smiley certainly had what it took and I can't recall anyone actually beating him in a sprint.

He raced people whenever and wherever they accepted his challenge. Sometimes we stopped traffic so that Smiley could race with someone. One time we were chilling on Wandsworth Road when we saw Jubert, one of the youngsters from the Hemans Estate. Jubert was mature for his age, and renowned for his gazelle-like agility in evading capture by the police. Smiley immediately challenged him to a sprint race. Jubert looked him up and down, sizing him up, and then eagerly accepted his challenge. The prize money was to be £100 and Smiley insisted that both he and Jubert give me their money to hold. You could always tell when the youngsters made money because they would flaunt it and then word would travel like wildfire. Whenever one of them made some money, you could be sure they'd receive a visit from the elders, who would lay claim to a cut of their earnings.

Jubert was balling (flush with cash) that day, and gave me his money very quickly while stating, "Be ready to give it back to me Ash, along with Smiley's hundred!"

Ironically, this was a day Smiley did not have £100 on him but he pulled out the theatrics and acted as if he was giving me his money. It worked well, because Jubert truly thought that Smiley had given me his money. £100 in the 70s was a lot of money so the atmosphere didn't take long to build up amongst the local youths. The noise was at its peak when one of them yelled, "Let's block the traffic!" The youths blocked off both ends of Thorparch Road, off the Wandsworth Road and as the race was about to take place, Smiley looked at me with such a confident expression that I knew he would win. He and Jubert took their positions on the side road. Jubert's friends were shouting for him, we were yelling for Smiley and the drivers caught in the blockade felt the energy and began beeping their car horns in anticipation. The race kicked off and Smiley took the lead immediately, but then Jubert seemed to find another gear and edged alongside him. Quick as a flash Smiley left him for dead and sprinted over the finishing line in first place. Jubert said it was Smiley's long legs that had won him the race.

He said to Smiley while breathing heavily, "You know it's because of your long legs, right?" Smiley took the money from me and replied, "You're not ready for this, but anytime you wanna go again, let me know!" That's how it went. Smiley challenged them, they agreed to it and he out-sprinted them. Naturally, he was smart enough to ensure that this particular talent also generated him some income.

Whilst we weren't really reaping in the money, we still knew that we had to keep up with trends somehow. One of the trends was to wear broad rim, trilby style beaver hats and Smiley and I had to get ours. We counted our money and calculated that we both had the same amount, which was £120. Beaver hats cost £110 each but that didn't deter us and before long, we'd each bought a beaver hat from Danny King in Acre Lane and had £10 left over. We were proud of our new headgear and showed them to everyone who was interested after returning to Lansdowne Green Estate. Out of nowhere, a tall black guy with an American accent appeared and said that he'd overheard us saying how much the hats cost. He said we were robbed and that he could get better beaver hats from the US for little or nothing.

He went on to tell us all about the luxuries that he possessed in America and became more interesting to Smiley and I with every word. He told us that his luggage had been delayed at the airport, and he didn't have any money until it was returned to him the next day. He said that if we loaned him some money he would see to it that we got beaver hats in abundance. We quizzed this guy for all it was worth but it wouldn't have mattered anyhow, because the temptation to get beaver hats was too much for us. We both gave him our last £10, and Smiley showed him where he lived so the guy could drop the money back the next day. Believe it or not, this guy did go back the next day but it was when Smiley was out and his mother was in. He gave such a speech to Smiley's mum that she gave him dinner on top of the money that Smiley and I had loaned him. He also took another £20 from Smiley's mother. What a conman! We didn't see this guy again until at least a year later when we were driving around the estate and Smiley said, "that looks like the guy who conned us." The difference being that he was dressed in full African attire while in deep conversation with a British couple. We pulled over the car and went over to him, taking care to remain inconspicuous. It was incredible as we heard him speaking in a full-blown African accent.

We decided to grab his attention by saying, "YOW – What you dealing with guy?" His facial expression let us know that we would have to fight with him if we went any further, and considering we were now thinking of Star Time and not wartime, we let it be.

After a while we took the beaver hat thing a stage further and designed beaver berets that only we could wear. Over time, we took loads of pictures in these berets until it reached a point where we couldn't be seen without wearing one of them. Smiley went into the dress code more deeply. He kept things as original as he could, and would always try different styles. I recall him doing an original tuck in socks thing when he wore tracksuits and boasting about it when others copied him.

It sounds amazing, but we even dressed stylish for the first Brixton riots. I remember driving through Brixton and seeing people pulling shop railings down while the police stood across the road and watched. By this time I was living with my mum in Brixton again, as my dad had predictably tired of my teenage antics and evicted me from his flat in South Lambeth Road.

It was a move that would come back to haunt him because my mum had been waiting for an opportunity to report him to the council for illegal occupancy and this was it. My dad had obtained the flat through a friend who had migrated back to the Caribbean and so my mum's intervention quickly ensured that he lost the tenancy.

When the riots happened in Brixton, I called Smiley to tell him what was going on and without any hesitation he replied, "Please pick me up dread, so we can do this..." I dressed accordingly in my army greens and picked Smiley up as quickly as I could. He'd also thought to wear army green and we laughed about it. We arrived in Bricky (Brixton), parked on the outskirts and made our way into the centre on foot. We were so excited, and couldn't believe the things we were seeing. The people on the streets were in charge and the police were all over the place, as if they were confused and waiting for orders. We stood at the top of Coldharbour Lane and witnessed some locals standing in the middle of the road while baiting a police car that was attempting to drive through. There were two officers inside and the driver was revving the engine as if threatening to plough into the crowd.

Eventually it took off and sped towards the people in the middle of the road but the barrage of bottles and bricks that rained down on their car forced them to crash and bail out. We couldn't see what happened after that but we were amazed at the levels some were willing to go to in this riot.

One youngster took the opportunity to assemble a pile of bricks, and he pelted every police car that passed. This young man had such feelings of vengeance towards the police that he didn't get involved with looting at all. Every time we passed the area he was in the same spot, and throwing bricks at passing police cars just about as hard as he could.

Another friend approached us and offered us the opportunity to take part in a serious mission, but after hearing the details Smiley and I wisely declined his offer. This friend wanted to build up a posse, storm Brixton police station and free the prisoners... Yeah right. He was very serious but out of at least thirty of us, only around three people joined him and this made him very upset. Although we were late arriving, Smiley and I went into some shops to see if there was anything left for us to take. I remember entering the electrical department of a store and seeing a man trying to take the last television from a shelf.

I put on a strong voice of authority and shouted, "LEAVE IT ALONE..." The man was so scared he darted off without even looking behind to see who it was and this is how we procured our first items from the riots. We went back and forth, dropping off goods and then returning for more. Smiley and I were proud of our achievements and spent many an hour bragging with other boasters from the riots about what goods we'd got that day. This was Thatcher's Britain, and she'd been encouraging us to make something of ourselves. She promoted free enterprise and it was pure freeness – thank you Maggie. My mum was totally against it but the hard continuous struggle she faced all her life and the temptation of a new television, handbags, shoes and clothes helped her to come to terms with those terrible days for Brixton retailers.

Chapter 2

Champion Sound

Time was moving on, but it was early days yet. Smiley was living in Union Grove with his girlfriend, and I was living with my son's mother in Clapham Common. We'd squatted in a flat in Battersea for several months before being evicted by Wandsworth Council, and the way we got on during that time assured us that we could live together. My mum played a big part in us getting the flat in Clapham Common with her specialised writing skills, as she wrote to the council and got their immediate attention. The flat was situated at the far end of the estate and virtually out of sight to most of the other residents, but we were still very popular. I played football with the younger youths, held music jams with them and entertained them with stories from my music travels. At this time I was blessed with two other children from two other women and so my concept was to tread lightly, mainly in the hope that I didn't slide on, or even fall through the thinly iced foundation I had created. I was often on tender hooks – sometimes just speaking with one of my other children's mothers brought implications at home, and especially if the news got there before me.

Champion Sound

Smiley and I reasoned with each other many times about the problems we kept facing with our women. However, I must admit that, thankfully and I mean thankfully, none of my women's problems escalated to the level that Smiley's did.

One morning I received a call informing me that Smiley had been admitted to St. Thomas' Hospital after being stabbed. The news shook me up and I remember sitting on my stairs with my head in my hands wondering what on earth was going on. I didn't know how badly he was injured or even if he was going to be alright but I prepared myself and got ready to visit the hospital. When I arrived at St. Thomas there was mayhem. People were shouting and holding each other back, whilst others were crying and screaming. I was confused and didn't know which way to turn. So many people were saying so many different things to me that I couldn't make head or tail of what was being said. To top it all everybody was shouting but as I looked around and steadied my focus, I eventually saw some faces that I recognised.

These people were from Brixton and although they were steaming angry and I already knew some of them to be rowdy, I took it as an opportunity to start the reasoning. I pulled one of them to one side and asked him what was going on. He told me that his girl cousin had been cut and the family was obviously not happy. I calmed him down best as I could and made my way into the emergency department. That's where I saw Smiley lying on a hospital *bed* with no *spread* and holding his *head*. At seeing me walk in, he said, "Dread, I've been stabbed in the lung." He looked tired and distraught but told me that he was okay, and was going to be alright. He said that both his girlfriends had been badly cut and he asked me to try and calm down one girl's family so they wouldn't harm the other girl he was living with. When I returned to the reception area, it looked like an aftermath of a demonstration that had got out of control and had escalated into a full-scale riot, although many of the people had already left and so the rumpus had died down. What happened? Well, Smiley had fallen for another girl while he was living at his girlfriend's flat. The other girl had obviously realised that Smiley was staying there and had paid him a visit early in the morning.

He told me that he was chilling at the flat when there was a knock on the door and his girlfriend went to answer. The next thing he heard was the sound of smashing glass and when he rushed to the front door he saw his girlfriend running towards the kitchen with blood streaming down her face. In her temper, the other girl had punched through the front door window and glass had flown everywhere, cutting Smiley's girlfriend's face quite badly. Smiley said that he'd tried to stop his girlfriend as she came rushing back out of the kitchen, with a big dutty knife. He said he believed that in her mad rage, she would have killed the other girl and so he did his best to hold her back but his girlfriend was too strong and cut the other girl before accidently stabbing Smiley in his side. This was not a good situation, and it had to be resolved. It was imperative that the other girl's family was reasoned with so there would be no repercussions. Smiley had his work cut out but to his credit, he did what he had to do and with his unique knack of wriggling out of tricky situations, even at the most difficult of times, he somehow brought an awkward situation to a close. At first I thought, 'damn that was bad, real bad' but then I looked on the positive side because at least the worst was over with.

I thought and somewhat hoped there could be no more major complications along our journey, or at least that's what I thought.

We're at the Hemans Estate in South London; the dance is packed and the audience in full swing when Smiley says to me, "Dread, go on the mic and nice this up". Whilst I hesitated and tried to think up excuses Smiley just went over, grabbed the mic and started to DJ. "Played by the champion sound with Smiley at the microphone, everyone come and gather round..."

Let me explain some reggae terminology here concerning the word "DJ," just so that people don't get it twisted. During those times a DJ was someone who'd address the crowd, and chant their lyrics into a microphone over instrumental tracks played in a dance or studio session, although nowadays the expression "DJ" usually refers to people who play music at gigs or on the radio. The word DJ eventually gave way to "MC" and then some people started to diss the term "DJ," saying that it meant "Dirty Jankrow" (dirty scavanger/vulture) and that MC stood for Master of Ceremony. Most people at that time weren't too overwhelmed by English DJs, who just weren't considered as good as their Jamaican counterparts.

This didn't worry Smiley as his confidence was immense, whereas I hated any sort of embarrassment. Other crew members and followers of the sound would try to encourage me by saying things like, "Your lyrics are great, so why don't you go on the mic?" or "I hope you're going on the mic tonight because I brought my whistle to blow down the place for you". Comments like those certainly helped me to overcome my fears to go on the mic in ram-jammed reggae dances. I felt like Popeye swigging back the spinach. In contrast, Smiley made sure you knew he was there, his spinach on hand at all times. He always made sure to send me massive shout outs as his sparring partner and as he used to say, "lyrical master."

Smiley had a distinctive lisp when he used to chat on the mic and this made some people underestimate his talent. Nothing deterred him though and he became better and better as we wrote lyrics galore, inspired by each other's styles. We wrote our lyrics anywhere and everywhere, rehearsed them at home and then tested them at dances. Buchanan often played in and around our local area and so we soon became recognised as good DJs, and truly enjoyed entertaining the audiences.

Champion Sound

Money wasn't a worry when we were chatting our lyrics and getting big forwards from Buchanan's faithful followers. Buchanan was our introduction into the mesmeric world of sound systems. To those lovely people who might think that I'm talking about the equivalent of a PA system when I refer to sound systems, please allow me to elaborate.

I'm talking about sound systems that were built from scratch by people attached to the sound, because everything was done by hand - from the carving of the wood used to assemble speaker boxes, to the inserting of speakers into them and then the painting of the boxes which was an art in itself, we duly accepted all of this as part and parcel of being a sound system member. We used to make silver metal cases in sizes of anything up to six feet long to hold the amplifiers, as it was a main part of a top sound system's agenda to possess very powerful amplifiers. The original amplifiers were valve amps that carried power of up to 600 watts each, and then came the transistor amps that could fire up even more power. Most sound systems would have three amps to drive their sound - one to drive the bass speakers; one to drive the midrange and one to drive the top treble section.

The amps would be wired to a pre-amp that was usually stationed on top of the amp case and next to a single turntable. Yes, a single turntable. There was no mixing on two decks, so you'd have to change or turn over that record as quickly as you could. There were no CDs either. Like every other sound-system we played vinyl - yes, records, and that came in the form of 7" and 12" discs. Most sound systems would carry a range of speaker boxes, holding 10" speakers for treble, 12 to 15" speakers for midrange and 15 to 18" speakers for the bass. The sound system members would distribute these boxes around the venue according to its size. For example, in a house dance they might use just one set of speakers in each room, but in a hall or larger venue they would place their sets of speakers in two or all four corners of the hall. Most sets of speakers would have the bass speakers at the bottom, midrange in the middle and treble at the top. The speaker boxes that were made for the bass section could have one, two, three or four speakers in them, depending on what the sound system members desired or could afford. The speaker boxes that held four speakers were called "Four Faces" and "House of Giants" and were designed to drop real serious and heavy bass.

Sound systems would shake up any venue they played at, vibrating the windows, wooden panels and anything that was not firmly fixed, even concrete. When a sound system played in a dance on its own, they'd play tracks and entertain the crowd with DJs chatting lyrics over the versions and instrumentals. But when a sound system was playing in a dance against or alongside a rival the format changed, and each sound system would be afforded a set time period to play their tracks until they handed over to the other one. Many a time there would be arguments over the mic between the sound systems' mic men about the length of time the other sound system played, who had the most exclusive dub plates, or which sound dropped the heaviest bass line. Sometimes the arguments would escalate into physical fights, and incidents involving knives and axes were not uncommon. This was a time before there was easy access to guns in the community, and so as I previously mentioned most people lived to tell the tales of their war days.

I remember one night in Brixton Town Hall when three sound systems – Moa Ambassa, owned by Beres Bassa; King Tubby's owned by Cecil, and Small Axe owned by Keithy Axe were playing against each other in a cup clash.

Smiley and I never actually chatted on Moa Ambassa, but it was one of our favourite sound systems. It was a Rasta sound and they appealed to us with their coordinated roots way of playing, so we were jamming in a corner of the Town Hall near where they were set up. The clash was going well and we were totally enjoying it until someone went on to King Tubby's mic and announced that, "Small Axe sound has been disqualified from the clash because they are full of distortion..." As soon as that statement was made, Keithy Axe made his way menacingly over to King Tubby's with an axe in his hand. Bob Marley's lyrics immediately came to mind. "If you are a big tree, I'm a small axe, aiming to cut you down...."

All we saw was pushing and shoving and then it kicked off. Axes were swinging and getting caught in speaker wires that were hanging from the ceiling, people were running and falling over each other and the elders were shouting at the top of their voices to try and gain some control. When it died down, Keithy Axe and his entourage made their way over to where we were standing with Moa Ambassa. Smiley and I were like, "oh shit..." Keithy told Beres that the clash was fixed and he wanted to play him again now down at The Hole in Landor Road.

Champion Sound

The Hole was in the basement of a West Indian food shop. Its entrance was a tiny door next to the shop that was advantageous to the hustlers and challenging for the police. The staircase was so narrow that it was impossible for two people to pass each other, while the floor space could hold around fifty or so people. Inside, it was so dark that when untoward incidents took place, no one knew who the perpetrators were. It could have easily been called "The Bunker," because whenever we raved there we were so oblivious to what was happening outside that World War III could have started and we still wouldn't have noticed. Beres Bassa looked Keithy straight in the eyes and replied, "Ah me win the cup, so just bring the cup..." Fortunately, no one was seriously hurt at the clash, but being around sound systems brought action on top of action, and ours was no different. Such dramas aside, the main goal was for our sound to be recognised for its musical qualities and heavyweight bass line, just like the top sound systems. Buchanan owned some powerful amps and speakers and on a scale of one to ten, with ten being the heaviest, I would say that our sound system would rate around seven in heaviness, while top sounds like Sir Coxsone and King Tubby's would easily rate ten on their day.

Champion Sound

Knowing that Buchanan wasn't the heaviest sound naturally didn't prevent us from thinking that we were the best sound in town. Buchanan was everything to Smiley and myself – this sound system was our master and anytime it called, no matter what else was happening, we had to be there.

As I said there wasn't much money running at the time but so long as we had Buchanan, everything was great as far as we were concerned. The energy was something else as we carried heavy-duty speakers, coils of wire and record boxes in and out of extremely awkward locations and conditions. Usually, all we received in return were cuts, bumps and bruises and yes, we complained all the time, but that's just how it was.

It was our love for the sound that drove us to stick it out day after day, month after month and year after year. It was in places called "shubeens" (all-night raves selling unlicensed alcohol), underground basement bunkers and squats where we developed and perfected our DJ skills. Squats were my favourite as it took careful planning and execution to locate an unoccupied flat or house, get in somehow and then find electricity to power our dance. The usual method involved replacing empty fuse boxes with those from neighbouring flats.

Most of the time, we got away with it and then we'd return the fuses to their original location in the early hours of the morning. Some neighbours believed there had been power cuts in their flats while others may have realised we'd taken their fuses, but were too afraid to complain. The laws regarding squatters' rights were different back then and the police were limited in what they could do whenever neighbours called them to the scene. The main thing they enforced was the noise factor so we would turn it down when asked, wait until they were gone and then blaze up that sound again. As Buchanan became more popular, the sound started to play further afield. We played in Railton Road on Brixton's famous front line and travelled out of town to places such as Nottingham. I must re-emphasise that the Buchanan era was a significant part of Smiley's and my development as DJs. We used to play against small sound systems like Killer Watt from Battersea and Small Axe No. 2 from the Patmore Estate, off Wandsworth Road. Small Axe No. 2 was the baby sound to Small Axe, a sound system that was made up of, let's just say, quite a few bad boys. That made us a bit cautious but it never stopped us from giving them a hard time with music and lyrical clashes.

Buchanan never backed down from clashes and some tough characters began to follow us. At one stage some people tried to brand Buchanan as thieves after a rival sound lost their dub plates one night, and some Buchanan followers just happened to be nearby. Something similar happened on another occasion when some speaker boxes and amps were stolen and again, some of our followers just happened to be nearby. One night we had to allow some of the elder boys from Small Axe No. 1 to look through our record box, just to prove to them that we were not the ones who broke into their van and stole their records. Another time another sound owner wanted to examine our amplifiers after claiming that we had stolen their sound system.

Smiley always enjoyed these sound clashes, and used intelligently structured rhymes to lyrically destroy other DJ's.

One night Buchanan was playing at an address on Paulet Road in Camberwell alongside a local sound system that featured two DJs from Brixton. Both of them were cheeky on the mic and why not? They were well known rude boys from town after all, but Smiley and I took the mic and launched into...

"We don't know much about history, don't know much about biology. We don't know much about psychology but all we know, dem can't DJ like we..." Uh-oh, that made those other DJs mad and they became threatening. Thankfully, the fracas was quickly squashed as there were a lot of people there who knew us.

"Sound tapes" – recordings of live dancehall sessions from Jamaica – were the in-thing, as they helped us to keep up-to-date with the origins of what we were doing. Smiley and I collected as many of these tapes as we could, and especially when they featured our favourite artists. When we heard lyrics that we rated as good, we wrote versions of them. For example, Smiley changed lyrics that went, "Mama coo, mama sa, mama coo, mama sa..." to "Supe a supe, car a car, me say train dat a train..." Whilst I changed lyrics that went, "Strictly rub a dub a me a play" to "Strictly Lucozade ah whe' me sip..." Artists from Jamaica like Brigadier Jerry, Nicodemus and U Brown were mashing up the scene at the time. Smiley's favourites were Brigadier and U Brown, whilst I was crazily inspired by Nicodemus. On one occasion Smiley impersonated U Brown and I impersonated Nicodemus just to try and check two girls.

We even faked the raw Jamaican accent and got the girls' phone numbers! Local people started to hear about our lyrical ability and this led to Smiley and I chatting on various sound systems in and around Brixton. Black Harmony was a sound that we used to chat on frequently when Buchanan was not playing out. It was owned by an elder by the name of Chinna, and helped give us the confidence we needed to entertain audiences that weren't so familiar with us. Supertone was another sound that helped us to conquer unfamiliar territory, and to develop our lyrics. Smiley knew Chubba, the owner of Stereograph from school and we would chat on their mic whenever we passed through their dances. We also chatted on King Tubby's – home of the legendary UK DJ Tippa Irie and talented Ras General Slater – quite a few times as the sound-system members were mostly close friends of ours.

We were fortunate to be able to chat alongside a number of local DJs and singers who were all talented in their own right – DJs like Ricky Ranking, who would chat on the mic from the beginning of the dance and go right through 'til morning. His lyrics were simple but effective, whilst his melodic delivery kept you entertained all of the time.

Lorna G was a female all rounder who could sing and DJ competently, and always generated maximum crowd appreciation and reaction with her well-delivered lyrics. Welton Irie was well respected for his mic ability, whilst Colonel Flux was his sparring partner and full of vibes. He had a flow and tone that oozed class and professionalism.

He and Welton Irie shared a mic on Front Line with Grandfather and Chucky, who was the king at hosting dances. Maestro was another daddy of the mic. He was very entertaining, and had a great sense of humour, whilst Marshall Lee led the fight against DJs who pirated lyrics. Other notable local DJs and singers from those days included Dego Ranks, Johnny Dollar, Champion, Sugar Dread, General T, Bikey Dread, Levi Roots (Mr. Reggae, Reggae Sauce), Jah Screechy, Waterloo, Colonel Boogie and Mikey Foreigner – a vibes DJ who always got the dance rocking with his big personality. There were others who I haven't yet mentioned, but respect equally since they all helped to bring the UK DJ and MC business to the heights it's at now. Up to this point, neither Smiley nor I had ever received any payment for our DJ talents.

Even after dances where we DJ'd lyrics all night and perspired until we lost weight, no one had thought us worthy of any financial reward until Skully came along. He was a short, stocky black youth from our area who owned a small electrical shop in Clapham, and he was a true admirer. Sometimes we would visit him at his shop and reason about lyrics and DJs for hours. When he told us that he played music at the Four Aces Club in Dalston and invited us to appear there, we accepted without hesitation. But it would be the first time that we performed out of town without our Buchanan contingency, and so it presented a real test for us. This would tell us if our lyrics were really as good as the locals said they were and more significantly, it would let us know if people who had never heard of us before would appreciate our style.

Four Aces was a popular club that guaranteed a full house and the night we performed there, it certainly lived up to expectations. Girls were in abundance and outnumbered the boys three to one. The atmosphere was electric and everyone was singing along as they partied. As we stood nervously waiting to be called on the small stage Smiley asked me, "What lyrics are you drawing?"

I told him that I was going to chat 'The Car Style' and he in turn told me that he was going to chat 'Cain and Abel'. 'The Car Style' and 'Cain and Abel' were the two lyrics that always got a positive reaction whenever we performed them to our faithful. Smiley decided on a last minute practice run and while trying not to make it obvious to onlookers, he began mumbling his 'Cain and Abel' lyrics. I followed suit and began to rehearse 'The Car Style' when the music suddenly stopped. We snapped to attention and heard Skully announce on the mic, "People, it's show time!" He called us up onto the stage and gave Smiley the mic who immediately started chanting, "I want to hear it from the sexy posse..." The girls went wild, and from there on until we finished chatting our two styles, the noise they made for us was deafening. It was definitely strong enough to stick firmly in my memory bank and was the highlight of our night so far but when Skully took us over to one side and gave us £5 each, we celebrated that moment as if we had won the lottery. This was our first ever payment for DJing on the mic.

It blew our minds and in the car driving home we bounced, pumped and laughed while making comments such as 'We are DJs who get PAID!'

It was when Smiley started to chat on Sir Coxsone and Front Line sound systems that his popularity on the underground sound circuit grew. Sir Coxsone used to play in a club in Battersea called Bennett's that had a see-through dance floor with piranhas swimming below. Yes, real piranhas. I was somewhat conscious of them whenever I skanked (danced) in that area. Girls would have the boys drooling over their sexiness as they modelled in rah-rah skirts, causing Smiley and I to shake our heads and say, "Raaa..." every five minutes in admiration. All the *guys* had their *eyes* on the girls *thighs*, but ultimately it was the piranhas below that viewed the full *prize*.

Hey, this was still early in our careers so I still had that little shy thing going but not Smiley. He went over to the mic and chatted his lyrics.

"Me can't tek me damn tailor
September me give him a thousand dollar
Me tell him fi mek a suit made to measure
Him never really screw, him say it's a pleasure
But him too out a order
Cos' when me try the suit, it was a disaster
Do it Jah, me say I will check him later

But whe' me say. When me come back the suit it hang up pon a rack.

The trousers like a shorts and the jacket like a Mack..."

In fact Smiley didn't only chat his own lyrics, but mine too. Lyrics like...

"Me and Shirley Beal could never do no deal

Me buy the girl gold, she say it don't look real

Me buy her silver, she say its stainless steel

She invite me round her yard to tek in a meal

But when me mek a move me say the gal start squeal.

Then she wriggle up her body like electric eel.

It's a good thing I Man get up and use the chair as a shield.

And deflect the flying high heel..."

It was always an honour for Smiley and I to chat on Sir Coxsone sound, as to us it was the sound with the longest and most prestigious heritage. Coxsone's history went back at least a decade before we came to the forefront so to chat on that sound and gain appreciation from their followers meant we must be doing something right.

Sir Coxsone himself, Festus, Blacker Dread, Jessus, Bikey Dread, Gappy Dread, Levi Roots, Jah Screechy, Wandan, Naphtali and Fathead were just a few of the names that formed this great set-up. Coxsone was a sound that we'd been hearing about from the time our eyes were at the same height as our knees, and so their encouragement meant so much to us. We used to chat on Coxsone sound at different venues and dances but when we went on their mic at People's Club in Paddington, it was the first time that we'd entertained the Jamaican contingency that used to follow Coxsone. General Saint and Clint Eastwood, two excellent entertainers from Jamaica, were among the audience and that made us quite proud as they showed us respect. We admired their style, had tapes of them and even saw them perform live on stage on Brixton's front line once, so it was super cool receiving respect from generals of the business such as these.

Sir Coxsone sound-system would always hold a special place in our hearts, even though we'd started to chat on other sounds by then. But Buchanan was our foundation, and it was only there that we felt completely relaxed on the mic.

The impact we were making around London triggered DJs from other sound systems to come to Buchanan, just so they could hear our lyrics or to chat on the mic with us. Junior started to invite Welton Irie and Flux to come over to the Buchanan dances from Front Line. We were well into writing original lyrics by then and although Welton and Flux were really popular at the time, they were still using lyrics borrowed from top Jamaican DJs. After Welton and Flux began to chat on Buchanan, we were eventually invited to chat on Front Line sound. Their dances were completely different to what we were used to and it took some time before we went near their mic. Welton and Flux used to call us "shy DJs" and subsequently devised a plan to get us to chat. I was standing near Flux while he was on the mic in one of their dances when suddenly he put the mic in my hand and said he's going to the toilet. It wasn't so bad at first because there was a vocal playing, but then Welton pulled up the track and indicated that he was going to play the version. He and Flux had planned to get me chatting on Front Line and it worked, so I just chatted the first lyrics that came into my head. "One, two, operator that a you. Fling whey part one and mek me give dem part two..."

I kept chatting until eventually the crowd kicked up in appreciation. Welton pulled up the track and someone gave me a flier to read over the mic. I tried to control the nerves in my voice but to no avail, my voice was trembling and I pushed the mic into Smiley's hand, who welcomed the opportunity to show his quality.

"Now people remember, it's my pleasure to bring to you a dance to treasure..."

Smiley's announcement about the forthcoming dance was so skilful, the crowd cheered as if he was chatting lyrics. We became officially invited guests on Front Line sound system after that, and would chat on their mic every so often. Front Line was the ultimate at the time, seeing how everyone in Brixton spoke about this sound like it was royalty. If you never went to a Front Line dance then you were not really a raver at all, and were classed as a 'rave novice'.

Sometime after we were chatting on Front Line sound, Welton and Flux had a dispute with Trevor, the owner of Front Line, and they stopped chatting on the sound for a while. Trevor approached us about teaming up more regularly and we started making bigger waves amongst the sound system circuit.

We would chat old lyrics, new lyrics, fictional and reality lyrics and the response that we received gave us that extra drive to take it even more seriously. It wasn't until we started to chat on Ladbroke Grove's front line that the hardcore Jamaican posse got the fullness of our lyrics and started rating us in a big way. It was an honour to know that the originators of the DJ business respected and appreciated what we did. Jamaican recording artists such as Ranking Dread and Errol Dunkley, and high-profile Jamaicans who were popular on the circuit such as Yardie Ron, Troubles and Jabbaduce all gave us maximum respect for our lyrics and styles. They even started to encourage us to go on the mic every time they saw us.

We were very appreciative of everyone's positive reactions but to be honest, we were bemused when faced with opposition from someone in Front Line's ranks. As ever, we had to take the rough with the smooth. We were returning from a Front Line dance in the countryside one night and upon entering the coach, we found that one of Trevor's faithful followers was in a foul mood. He was an elder and the brother of one of those famous Brixton mic veterans.

He looked over at Smiley and snarled, "You're rubbish. You're no good as a DJ, you cannot step in Welton and Flux's shoes, and you'll never make it..." Then he briefly turned to me in the meantime, "Asher, you might have one little chance with that car style thing you've got, but SMILEY YOU WILL NEVER MAKE IT..." The youths on the coach hit out against what he'd said, and told him that he must be mad; that Smiley had got wicked lyrics and they're all original. Need I say more? Yes, I think I will! Because "Mr. Unbeliever" subsequently apologised, and admitted to Smiley on more than one occasion that he was wrong. Both of us truly believed that we were the best DJs around.

Everyday we were over at the flat in Union Grove, writing and rehearsing lyrics like crazy and so you can imagine our disappointment when we heard that Sir Lloyd was holding a DJ Explosion event at the Dick Shepherd School in Tulse Hill, and hadn't asked us to perform. Now a DJ Explosion is a live stage event featuring a host of DJs who are popular on the circuit, and each of them would be invited on stage to perform their lyrics.

Champion Sound

It wasn't a competition but this event was being recorded for a live LP and this brought a real competitive edge to proceedings. As far as I am aware this was the first UK DJ Explosion of its kind and the DJ and sound system community was ecstatic about it. It hurt our feelings that we wouldn't be appearing, and the only way we knew how to react was to play the whole thing down as if it meant little or nothing to us. At first we insisted that we wouldn't even attend but on the day, we had to go. Dick Shepherd had already hosted many sound system dances but I had never seen anything like the sort of crowd that was there that evening. As we approached the entrance, it was complete mayhem. Pushing and shoving had replaced any attempts at organisation and the crowd's backward and forward momentum brought back memories of the times when I was in a football crowd, trying to head towards opposing fans. Smiley was never phased by crowds and told me to, "keep close dread" as he pushed forward toward the entrance. As we got closer I could see some of the main guys from Brixton's front line trying to manage the chaos. One or two brandished wooden clubs or had dogs, and none of them were holding back in their mission to resume order.

Eventually, Smiley's height came into play and worked to our advantage. After a while he was spotted and one of the guys called on a few others to clear an opening for us, so we could enter. Inside, it was even more packed than outside. No one could move freely and so it was another task for us to make our way into the dancehall. Slowly but surely, we inched as close to the stage as possible, so we could get a clear enough view of the performers. It was the lyrics of Peter King, from Saxon sound system that really stood out for us that night. When we heard him chat those lyrics and saw the crowd's tremendous reaction, we could only look at each other and ask, "What did he do?" We'd just witnessed what people will call "the fast style" – yes, that same old '80s' lyrical style that ultimately helped UK DJs, MCs, "spitters" or whatever they're called now to become what they are today.

We were getting increasingly popular on the sound system scene but then some other DJs started to diss us verbally. People would approach us and say there is a DJ called Champion from Clapham who chats on a sound called Jamdown Rockers alongside General T and singer Sugar Dread.

People let us know without any bars held that Champion says he's better than Asher and Smiley, and that he will bury us with lyrics. Smiley found this amusing and used to send back messages to say that anytime Champion's ready for us, then we're ready for him.

When it came to other sound systems and their DJs, we made it our duty to know all about them. It didn't matter whether they came from Jamaica, America or England – once we heard about them, we'd carry out our research. We listened to tapes, asked people for their opinions and went to hear some of the UK sound systems play live. We'd already heard about this sound Saxon and their very lively DJ Papa Levi, and so we listened to a tape of them and Jamdown Rockers with big expectations. The tape certainly made us laugh as it had Papa Levi and Champion going at each other with battle lyrics. Papa Levi chat a lyrics that went, "Champion the wonder horse. Hee-haw" which had the crowd going crazy. Champion hit back with hard lyrics that also gained appreciation but it was Papa Levi who captured our attention. It was the first time that we'd actually heard a UK DJ with such a unique lyrical technique.

He was exciting, had extreme clarity and his lyrics were delivered with tight precision on the rhythms. We also took note of the fact that he was very cheeky, and a fearless microphone technician. Little did we know or even anticipate that further down the line we would be starring alongside this DJ on Saxon sound system, and even entertaining audiences around England.

Chapter 3

Continuous Rhyming

Smiley and I were listening to a clash tape that featured the late great Nicodemus and some other great Jamaican DJ's. Smiley rated the Jamaican DJ legends Brigadier Jerry and U Brown in a big way but, like me he was mesmerised by Nicodemus' deep tone of voice, smooth lyrical flow and intelligently structured rhymes. Nicodemus was special in my eyes and I was glad that Smiley felt his energy too. The man's lyrics were of a serious nature but they were also clever and funny, and his rhymes lasted twice as long as the usual three or four lines – all of which made him exceptional.

Demus' voice came in again and got our attention immediately. "Me mash it in a country and me mash it in a town. Me skin is very black, say I man don't brown. Me weigh one hundred and thirty five pound. Me tell you Jack Ruby ah the number one sound..."

Demus went on like that, but after around seven lines he changed the rhyme and stopped, leaving Smiley and I frustrated. We'd be saying, "Why did he stop the rhyme man?" and "Those lyrics were proper. He should have continued rhyming!"

Continuous Rhyming

Rhyming meant that every stanza or line had to end in the same phoneme (different words which sound the same) such as "time" and "sunshine." Nicodemus was an expert at rhyming and this inspired us massively. We felt unfulfilled when he changed the rhyme on that tape and that gave us the idea to lengthen our own rhymes. We began to test our writing capabilities by writing longer lyrics until eventually we established what we called 'Continuous Rhyming'. People were amazed at how long we could keep rhyming and they always yelled out in appreciation after maybe fifteen or so lines. This wasn't easy to maintain and it was an even bigger challenge to maintain the same phoneme throughout the whole lyric while still chatting intelligent, constructive lyrics. For two young fresh minds like ours, it was all very exciting. Sometimes we wanted to get across so many lyrics on the one track that we would only have room to put a chorus at the beginning, but at other times we wouldn't even have a chorus at all. We enjoyed testing ourselves with how far we could go with our continuous rhyming style, as heard on Smiley's 'Cain and Abel' and my own 'The Car Style' – lyrics that we'd written during our time on Buchanan, and that set the standard for those we'd write throughout the rest of our journey.

Continuous Rhyming

"Cain and Abel sat around the table.

Cain said to Abel, 'beg you pass me an apple.'

When I was a youth I used to read up me Bible.

Now me turn a man me just turn Jah disciple.

Me pray fi the fit – me pray fi cripple.

Ca some say me cute becah me have dimple.

Me sweeter than the sugar man, me sweeter than treacle.

Before me mek coffee, me have fi boil me kettle.

Me know when it boil because it have to whistle.

I man don't fool. I man sensible.

Some say me mad, but me mind stable.

That's why me drive a car and me no ride bicycle.

Me eat up me steak and me vegetable.

And when me done dat, a strictly apple crumble.

Daddy Culture don't thief, Daddy Culture hustle.

Any money that me get, me just mek it double..."

And so on. Smiley made his name with lyrics like those, and here are some from my own continuous rhyming tune, 'Car Style'.

"Asher know everything 'bout the car – me a go show you that star.

97

Continuous Rhyming

Cha, Accelerator – speedometer.

Indicator – window wiper.

The cigarette lighter – carburettor.

Alternator, don't forget the oil filter.

Distributor – starter motor.

The master cylinder – disc brake calliper.

Yes, the regulator which connect to the heater.

It have four tyre, a timing chain tensioner.

Yes, the regulator which ah circulate the water.

Shock absorber and engine ventilator.

It have air cleaner, front and rear bumper.

The condenser – tank unit sender.

Rear brake compensator – temperature tranducer."

Those lyrics were written around 1981, then in the mid-1980's a DJ on Jamaica's leading sound Kilimanjaro named Burro Banton came with the smash hit 'Boom Wah Dis,' which he'd written using the same continuous rhyming style that Smiley and I had established. Another veteran Jamaican DJ called Johnny Ringo came with a style around the same time where he began by saying, "Jah man, Jah man, Jah man, me a go kill you wid E".

Continuous Rhyming

Every one of his lines ended in "E" and this caught on rapidly amongst Jamaican and UK DJs but it still wasn't the complete package of continuous rhyming since the rhyming stopped after a while. Smiley and I had set it so that our lyrics not only maintained one phoneme from start to finish, but they easily lasted as long as the rhythm tracks. Examples of our continuous rhyming styles can be found on YouTube. They include 'Shan a Shan', 'Slam Bam Jah Man', 'Roots Reality' and 'Entertainer-Entertainer' – all by Smiley Culture – and also my own 'Asher In Court', 'Bubble Wid I', 'Rule Over England' and 'Lyrics Protecting'. However, the biggest and most significant example of our continuous rhyming style is Smiley's hit track 'Police Officer' because once he's finished with the introduction, he stays on the same phoneme right through to the end.

We went to People's Club in Praed Street, Paddington on Smiley's birthday one year to rave it out. People's Club was definitely one of the clubs of the time and every hardcore raver from that era must have gone there at some point. There was a small reception counter with a cloakroom behind it and a door at the bottom of the stairs that acted as a security measure.

Continuous Rhyming

A narrow staircase led down to the dancehall, which was luxurious. There were two small platforms where the sound systems would set up, and a carpeted floor that afforded dancers a degree of comfort as they danced all night. The seating and tables in the V.I.P area were top class as well. Like I said, every real raver went to people's Club. You had north, south, east and west London people all claiming it as their own favourite raving spot.

Visiting Jamaicans, who we called "yardies" were no different. They too, took the People's Club into their hearts and regularly raved there. They formed their own party corner near the toilets at the far end of the dancehall where they would make the most noise while having the best time. Whenever a new yardie with any kind of status came over from Jamaica you would be sure to know about it if you raved at the People's Club. It was a given that their name would be called on the mic as a form of greeting from the UK DJs. Sir Coxsone and Front Line sound systems were playing the night of Smiley's birthday and the People's Club was in full swing. Welton Irie and Flux were still in dispute with Trevor and so they went over to Coxsone instead.

Continuous Rhyming

The crowd was used to the two DJs performing on Front Line and so they were shocked to see them on Sir Coxsone – added to which, they were still chatting well-known DJs' lyrics. Trevor boldly announced that now was the time for original lyrics and he called for us to come up and show everyone what we could do. Smiley said to me, "Come on dread, go mash this up for my birthday" and I obliged.

Front Line's younger DJs were holding the mantle that night. Starsky was around fourteen years old and Joe 90 a mere twelve, but the maturity they displayed on the mic earned them the full respect of the people. Joe 90's young voice made my own voice sound well developed by comparison. If you listen to his concrete voice nowadays you may not believe this, but I can assure you that it's true and I still have the old TDK cassette of this dance to prove it. From he handed me the mic I performed a range of continuous rhyming lyrics, from my popular 'Car Style' to lyrics that went...

"How do you use a public telephone?
You pick up the receiver you listen fi a sound.
The sound whe you hear, dat a dialling tone.

When you hear dat, you spin the numbers dem around. And
when you get an answer you push your money down.
If you talk long, you end up spend off nuff pound..."

The crowd loved every minute and knowing that Welton and
Flux were over on Coxsone Sound, they got behind me even
more enthusiastically than usual. Things got heated after I
lyrically smashed up the dance and so I refused to go back up
when it was Front Line's time to play again.

Trevor was calling for me on the mic, urging me to, "Come
back up and show them more original lyrics!" I could see that
he had a secondary agenda, which was to humiliate Welton
and Flux as much as he could. I wasn't feeling that because
Welton, Flux and I had built a good friendship. I certainly
didn't want to jeopardise my friendship with them, or make it
look like as if I was taking advantage of their situation with
Trevor. Smiley naturally, would have none of it. He went on
the mic, reminded everyone in the club that it was his birthday
and lyrically smashed up the place with the likes of 'Tell Me
What You Want Fi Your Birthday', 'Tell Me What You Want Fi
Your Wedding' and the now legendary 'Caine and Abel'.

Smiley then called up Willie Major, who continued to smash up the place with lyrics like, "Mi name Willie Major, a new entertainer. "Me spar with Asher and the one Smiley Culture, fa dem a me teacher..." Smiley grabbed the mic from Willie Major and stated loud and clear. "It's a shame on imitators, this DJ has only been chatting for a few months, it's a shame on imitators, it's a shame..."

Smiley then called me back up, and I couldn't resist any further. We then performed our continuous rhyming in combination, taking each line in turn.

Asher: "Me have the sling shot."
Smiley: "Me have the rock."
Asher: "Up upon the hill top."
Smiley: "Deso we a block."
Asher: "We put fi the rock."
Smiley: "Up in the sling shot."
Asher and Smiley together: "And any imitator that pass fi spot."
Asher: "Elastic pull back."
Smiley: "Fi him head we a clock."
Asher: "Man we lick couple shot."

Smiley: "And we lick off him hat."

Asher and Smiley together: "We lyrics dem go on like a train pon a track. Chiggity-chiggity-chiggity hoo. Chiggity-chiggity-chiggity chack..."

On and on we went, alternating line for line in a continuous rhyme for so long that the crowd yelled out in appreciation. If we thought that we were big before, well now we thought we were real stars, but these were early days yet.

Chapter 4 –

Leggo Mi Hand

There were nights when we would travel all around Brixton and the surrounding areas in search of dances where we could go on the mic and entertain the people there. We would see other DJs, like Marshall Lee, who were on the same tip.

Marshall depicted mission-like qualities in his personality and mic ability so he used to roar out at us on the way past, "Me just mash up a dance round the corner rude bwoys, and me a go mash up a next one round the next corner right now!"

If by any chance we found a little more time to speak to each other we would ask Marshall where the dance was that he'd mashed up and in turn we would tell him where the dance was that we'd just demolished. Attending every dance that we possibly could not only helped to boost our popularity, but also maintain and improve our DJ craft.

Smiley hated paying to get into dances or raves and went out of his way in adhering to his principles. In Brixton it appeared that nearly all the youths had a presumptuous attitude when it came to paying to get into a dance or rave. So many just didn't do it.

Bad boys didn't want to pay because they were hard and insisted that they didn't have to. Weed sellers didn't want to pay because they wanted respect for providing in-demand products to the community. Hustlers didn't want to pay because they believed the amount of drinks they'd buy for the night warranted their free entry. Sound system members didn't want to pay even though their sound wasn't even playing at the venue and most obvious of all, every artist didn't want to pay because a dancehall code had built up over the years that stated artists should get into every dance without paying. To me, that's the most obvious reason why someone shouldn't have to pay to enter a dance because a good artist is always likely to be requested to do something on the mic. Many of the promoters who were around at that time acknowledged this, and allowed popular artists free entry into their dances.

Smiley thrived on entering every dance for free. Even if it was a real tight affair on the door and the security personnel were handling their business robustly, Smiley would still try and get free entry for as many of us as possible.

It became a matter of principle for both of us, although sometimes when the doormen were definitely not having it, Smiley would get angry and make threats towards them. I'm sure some of these doormen felt aggrieved, and that made them even more determined to try to charge Smiley whenever he appeared at the door and wanted to get in their dances. As far as we were concerned, we were popular DJs who were getting respect around the community for our mic skills and lyrical prowess. We still weren't the superstars we dreamt of becoming however, and so looking back now I can understand why some doormen found it upsetting to let us in without paying. We were falling into disrepute with these doormen more and more frequently, and it was turning into a joke since we believed that some doormen simply had it in for us.

As we walked up to certain dances you could see some doormen adjusting their positions and adapting a more antagonistic stance. This only gave Smiley fuel for his tank and you could tell right away from the way he approached them that commotion was guaranteed.

Our approach as we strode towards the Sting dance on Somerleyton Road in Brixton was calculated and direct.

Me, Smiley, Mikey, Fox and a few other friends knew that we would face opposition from this particular doorman who we'd previously embarrassed. We'd resisted his demands that we should pay to get in the last dance he'd worked at, and he hadn't liked it one bit when due to the promoter's intervention, we'd all entered for free. "You got away with it this time," he'd snarled, "but any other dance I'm at, you lot are paying to get in!"

There's little doubt that his negative attitude towards us had something to do with the way Smiley just brushed past him at the door, not saying a word or even acknowledging him in any way.

Ultimately, he shouldn't have let that upset him, but just joined the queue of the many who voiced similar qualms about Smiley. A few people, including some of his old school friends, used to complain to me, saying that he walked past them without even saying hello. I always made the excuse that he probably never noticed them but they instinctively rejected that, saying things like, "Asher, he definitely saw me!"

Smiley's confidence mixed with his arrogance made him untouchable in his eyes and he didn't care whether people liked him or not, except we knew that getting round this particular doorman was going to be a real examination of our characters. We didn't know the promoter either, so the odds were against us from the off. We were still committed and unswerving in our mission to get into this dance without paying however. Our plan was to walk with swagger and purpose, so by the time we arrived at the dance gate we would already have built up a head of steam. The overall intention was to overpower the gateman and pass him so quickly that he wouldn't even know who we were. As we neared the gate and gathered pace, I felt a shudder through my body. It was a chilly night and the breeze was sharp. My ears were already cold and stinging like an elastic band was being flicked against them. Smiley caught a glimpse of the doorman and said, "There he is, let's do this!" We blended into the crowd that was assembled at the door and hurriedly pushed through while repeatedly saying, "Artists, artists, let the artists through!" It's funny, we found that approach always worked as people tended to accommodate us and move aside before they realised what was actually happening.

When we reached the door the doorman was occupied, searching someone. Smiley went past him in a whisper but before I could follow, the doorman quickly spun around and blocked the rest of us at the door. He said as loud as he could, "None of you are coming in here tonight without paying!" Immediately, the guys at the back started pushing forward, forcing me into this hulk of a doorman, my short height ensuring that my face was rammed into his midriff. He reacted wildly and with an eruption of energy, tried to push us back as best he could. It was to no avail however, and the sheer force of the posse's momentum forced him back into the passageway. We were in. Zoom, zoom, zoom... Everyone grabbed the opportunity and darted into this already jam-packed house dance. I made my way upstairs and found Smiley on the first floor talking to a girl at the top of the stairs. He looked at me and said apologetically, "I was asking her if she knew where the promoter was". The thought of reprisals from the doorman weighed a little heavily but every time I looked across at Smiley he was having such a good time dancing to the music, drinking Ribena and smoking sensimilla that it put my mind at ease. Plus, every now and again he would reiterate, "Pussy hole doorman!"

We raved for around five hours and at approximately 6 am, we decided that it was time for us to leave. I was conscious of the fact that the doorman still posed a threat and I'm sure Smiley was too. When we got downstairs and made our way out of the dance there he was standing outside, wearing the angriest expression you can imagine. We didn't need anyone to tell us that he was furious, because it was obvious. The only thing missing was the fire breathing out of his nostrils. Smiley instantly jumped at the chance and said to him, "Yow rude boy, don't tell me you were out here with that expression all night?" Everyone laughed and that left the doorman in a more awkward position. He dared not exercise any physical retribution because he was outnumbered and to top it all he knew Smiley's elder brother Rocky, whose reputation would make anyone back off. This doorman was just one out of a host of bouncers and gatemen who tried to make life difficult for us at dances. Don't get me wrong, lots of gatemen were cool with us but there were some who seemed determined to suppress our rights as artists to enter dances free of charge. After a while it became an addiction for us because the more dances we lyrically mashed up, the more dances we wanted to enter for free.

On a few occasions, Smiley even grew frustrated with me because of my equanimity when dealing with gatemen. I remember one particular time when we had entered a dance after a torrid encounter with some doormen. Smiley was still furious with them and he uncontrollably continued his rant at me. "Don't deal with them so nice man, they're disrespectful" he yelled, his temper blinding him from the fact that we were surrounded by people. I yelled back with something like "Who are you talking to?" and walked off in a huff. We both found separate spots to stand in the dance, but it wasn't long before Smiley came over and asked me if I wanted a drink. I accepted and things were back to normal in a flash. We were still Asher and Smiley, Batman and Robin... You get the drift.

Chapter 5

Saxon Invasion 1983

In every ghetto with a black community during the early '80s it was the same scene. On any given night from Thursday through to Sunday in community halls, or in the living rooms of countless council flats, thousands of teenagers would gather in spliff-fumed rooms and rock out to the latest beats, hot off the press from the studios in Kingston, Jamaica. They'd rock out to serious bass lines, thumping out of wardrobe sized speaker boxes... This was our disco, and there were as many sound systems as Sunday league football teams, all asking, 'how do we distinguish our sound? How do we break away from the pack and become a top-rated sound system?'

Smiley once mentioned that a friend he'd known from an early age called Dennis Rowe was in charge of Saxon sound system. He said that Dennis had invited him to chat on Saxon, but nothing had materialised as yet. One night, he and I were at Dick Shepherd listening to Stereograph sound system. Smiley had just finished bussing some lyrics and I was complimenting him for his performance when someone ambushed him. From their interactions I could tell he was an old acquaintance.

The man's behaviour towards Smiley was respectful but the way he was dressed and his hardcore expression had me thinking, 'this must be a real bad boy!' He was a dark-skinned youth with rough looking clothes and uncombed hair, with a cap dangling off to the side. Not only that, but he was accompanied by a few hard looking guys which led me to assume that this was a link from Smiley's time in lockdown. It was Dennis Rowe and as Smiley introduced us, I tried to recall if Smiley had previously said they were old school friends, or maybe cellmates. Dennis was direct and got straight to the point. "Bruv, none of them sounds can test Saxon, because when you hear my sound you're gonna know it's the best sound ever. Those other sounds are rubbish I'm telling you, because Saxon is the best..."

For the small amount of time that we spoke, Dennis must have mentioned Saxon and pointed out how great they were, around one hundred, twenty seven and a half times. The half came right at the end of the dance, when he was interrupted in mid-sentence by the hall lights coming on. Finally, he invited us to hear Saxon for ourselves. We thanked him for the invitation but never followed it through at the time.

However, circumstances dictated that we would eventually find ourselves in the corridors of the Saxon elected.

The Ace Club in Brixton, later known as The Fridge but now operating under the name Electric, was the venue chosen to hold a dance that featured DJs from different sound-systems. Smiley and I were there to witness a great night of live entertainment. Local DJs like Ricky Ranking, Lorna G, Champion, Dego Ranks, Johnny Dollar, GT and Horseman were smashing up the place. Loud whistles filled the air, the crowd was bubbling and everything was looking good until Dennis Rowe came over to us and told us that his DJs hadn't turned up. He was looking agitated and said, "I'm stuck man, and Saxon's meant to be appearing". In a charismatic tone he then said, "How about you two representing Saxon?"

The word 'No' came out of our mouths simultaneously, but Dennis wasn't deterred. He persevered until we crumbled under his persistently persuasive abilities. We finally agreed to go on stage to represent Saxon. At this point the host was giving Saxon DJs a final call to come on stage, so in a hurry, we walked across the middle of the dance floor and shouted to the host whilst jumping onto the stage from the front.

That was our second mistake for the night – the first was accepting the challenge in the first place. That's because the South London sound system scene was tribal and territorial, so two Brixton DJs chatting in Brixton on a sound system from Lewisham just didn't sit well with the home crowd. The only thing I can gain comfort from was that the crowd didn't boo us – they just kept very quiet. Now remember the place was loud just before we went on stage and so quietness was still not good. We had friends and family there and also girls that we liked, and so it was a bad night all round.

After the dance, we parked outside Smiley's girlfriend's flat, stayed in the car and spoke seriously about never DJing again. We spoke about the embarrassment and every time one of us mentioned another person who was there, we shuddered with awkwardness. We reasoned for at least four hours until we eventually said, 'Let's go home and sleep on it.'

The next day I still felt the burden hanging over me, and Smiley was the same. The only way we could deal with facing people was to ensure we were together handling the people's reactions as one.

A few days after the event we decided to be brave and take a walk out on the front line - Railton Road. To our amazement, nearly everyone was playing our section of the event on tape and saying how we had the best lyrics that night. Our part of the tape was void of any crowd noise so fortunately for us, they could hear our lyrics properly. What a confidence boost! We regained some self- belief and were ready for the next task ahead, the DJ Explosion at Riverdale Centre in Lewisham where nearly all the popular UK DJs would be performing.

The extravaganza's lead promoters were Dennis himself and Maxi Priest, and the date was the 15th of April 1983. It was shaping up to be a massive show and we took the build-up to it more seriously than ever before. I was contemplating changing my name from Asher Dread but couldn't find a name that I felt comfortable with. I had trimmed off my dreadlocks at the beginning of 1983 and felt that my name needed to change, especially the "Dread" part that I used as my surname. When I informed Smiley, he held council one evening and a few of us sat at his girlfriend's flat suggesting all sorts of DJ names for me.

The names stemmed from Asher Sinatra to Peter Saint but none of them actually sat well with me and so we continued until way into the evening. Then who else but Smiley said "Senator Asher"? It had a ring to it although I still had reservations but then when Smiley suggested I use the Senator part as the surname that was it – it sat nicely within my spirit and so my DJ name became Asher Senator.

A week before the big show at Riverdale, Dennis invited us to a Saxon dance so we could meet the team. When we were there Dennis brought over Peter King, who'd chatted those hot lyrics at Dick Shepherd's DJ Extravaganza – you know, the ones that got Smiley and I wondering what the fuck had just happened. When we were introduced, straightaway Peter King said to Smiley accusingly, "I heard that you stole my lyrics". This was definitely not the case, because Smiley was writing some serious lyrics at this stage. Smiley asked him 'what lyrics?' and Peter King said, 'Me Neat, Me Sweet'. Smiley said 'okay, chat it now'...

"Me neat me sweet me know how fi do it.

Me wash me hands me wash me feet.

Me brush me teeth me comb me hair.

Me eat me bulla wid me pear. Me gwan clear everywhere, do you hear?"

He delivered these lyrics at a rhythmic fast pace. Veteran Jamaican DJs such as U Roy, I Roy, Ranking Trevor, U Brown and others would speak fast in a hosting style on the rhythm but Peter King had chat fast in a rhythmic style, a speed chatting that we'd never heard before. We now understood why the audience had erupted at Dick Shepherd.

Nevertheless, the entirety of these lyrics were five to six lines, delivered in a very catchy style, but at the time we categorised it as a classy gimmick and said we needed to bring more lyrics to the table. When Smiley and I left the dance we decided to write two fast styles of our own. In fact, we said we would write even faster lyrics to counteract the accusation of pirating Peter King's lyrics. I wrote 'Me Short, Me Smart' with quite fast lyrics and Smiley wrote 'Slam Bam' which was even faster.

We kept the chorus pattern that Peter King had used but changed the lyrical delivery, making sure it was in our usual pattern of continuous rhyming. So ultimately, Peter King originated the fast style but we transformed it with our continuous rhyming lyrics.

Saxon Invasion 1983

Many connoisseurs of the UK DJ business are of the opinion that the fast style, coupled with continuous rhyming, was the game-changer that finally brought global recognition to UK DJs.

The Riverdale Centre was ram-packed with people on the night, and all DJs were requested to perform a little bit of their lyrics to the audience before the main show started. Smiley and I sang pieces of our fast styles. I started with this...

"Me short me smart, me know how fi talk.

Me walk, me talk with Jah love in me heart.

Me drive a car, no push no cart.

Ev-er-ry-day, I man take a bath.

Me no trust no shadow after dark.

So me don't skylark in no park.

Cos sea has shark, and tree have bark.

Bottle with cork, and knife wid fork.

Coke have froth, Noah built the Ark.

Some write it wid pen, some write it wid chalk.

Asher Sen-ee-ta the top of the chart..."

Then Smiley came with...

"Slam bam, Jah man, se hear dem fashion.

Me strong me long, me at the mic stand.

See in me ring, me wear diamond.

And from a youth I've been a car man.

Me drive Volvo and Mini Club Man

Me drive a Lancia and now me's a man.

Me full up a lyrics and education,

Who drive the most jeep? Must soldier man.

Who have the most Rover? Must Babylon..."

When it came closer to the actual show time, Smiley and I became more nervous. We still had the unpleasant memory of that event at the Aces Club so before it was time to go on, we found a quiet spot somewhere backstage and prayed to the Almighty, Creator of Heaven and Earth and the Universe and asked Him for His blessings.

This show was going to be a decisive moment in our DJ careers because it would determine whether or not we would carry on. The host called Smiley out first and he performed his three lyrics, including his roots lyric 'Cain and Abel'. The crowd gave him a good reception and I felt quite relieved, watching from backstage.

The host called me next and I performed my three lyrics, the most significant being 'Bam-Bam seven million: the biggest robbery in a England...'

Those lyrics worked so well with the crowd because a few days before there had been a seven million pound robbery that was splashed all over the media. When I came off stage Smiley hugged me and we laughed and joked, not just for the excitement of doing so well but also for the relief of not doing bad. Our joy was then boosted further when Papa Levi took to the stage and credited us for our performance. Remembering our prayer, we thanked the Almighty for having fulfilled it and so now more than ever, our DJing had purpose because after being so well received, we said to each other "Now we are DJs". The funny thing is we didn't bother to chat our fast styles for our main performance, because we didn't want people to think or say that we were dependant on anyone else's style.

Soon after the Riverdale Centre event, Saxon was due to play at a small venue in Deptford called Childers Street and so we decided to chat our new lyrics there. When we performed our long versions of Peter King's fast style the crowd was ecstatic, and that certainly made us feel more than welcome at Saxon.

Saxon Invasion 1983

Papa Levi, Daddy Colonel, Stout and Waterhouse were the main performers while Pinky Loo joined us on the mic, having just returned from a long spell in "foreign." That's anywhere outside South London that you travel to by boat or airplane, including the Isle of Wight. Peter King wasn't there that night but other DJs were and so we still made it a great night of entertainment. Smiley chatted some continuous rhyming styles with lyrics like...

"England so cold all me feel a ice breeze.

More time it come in like it's below naught degrees.

Me have fi tek caution with me car, put in anti freeze.

No want wake up in the morning try fi start it and it cease.

Man mek money, honey's made by the bees.

The mice live in dem hole, while the bird live in dem trees.

If me say you have chigger, might as well just say fleas.

England is a country with nuff venereal disease..."

Then I came in with...

"In the animal kingdom you find lion, you find tiger.

You find leopard and you find jaguar.

You find cougar and the Black Panther.

123

You find scavenger like the hyena.

You find elephant and you find zebra.

You find deadly spider like the tarantula.

You find crocodile and the alligator..."

Continuous rhyming became an instant hit with the Saxon DJs and things began to move forward progressively. The great talent that was around Saxon enabled them to adapt to changes and new trends easily, and so it was no surprise to hear the "top of the range" lyrics that Saxon DJs started to write. Saxon sound system was blessed with some of the most talented reggae artists in the country. In addition to Peter King the fast style originator, and Papa Levi the squadron leader there was Daddy Colonel, the roll tongue master. Tippa Irie, the lyric maker joined us further down the line and then those two lyrically gifted stylists, Rusty and Sandy. At full strength, Saxon also had two great singers – Roger Robin and Maxi Priest – as well as the highly rated female DJs Miss Irie (bless her soul), who was Tippa Irie's sister and Sister C. It was amazing to us that no Saxon DJs had written their own adaptations of Peter King's fast style before we came along, however when they finally did, it set a serious precedent.

Papa Levi delivered his version of the fast style and came with 'Mi God Mi King', which as you all should know, brought him international stardom. Every time Levi chatted 'Mi God Mi King' it got such a wild reaction that Maxi Priest and Barry Boom, a lovers' rock singer from the reggae group One Blood, took him in the studio and put it out on an independent label. 'Mi God Mi King' proved so popular that all available record presses in London had to run at full pelt to keep up with demand. The record was then picked up by Sly & Robbie's Taxi label in Jamaica and 'Mi God Mi King' made history by becoming the first record by a British artist to reach No. 1 in the Jamaican reggae charts.

We'd noticed the way Saxon's mic section always sounded crystal clear and loved chatting on it. This was thanks to Muscle Head, Saxon's co-owner and selector. As his name implies, Muscle Head was a solid built, muscular man of few words, and the archetypal strong, silent character. He could have walked straight out of a Clint Eastwood western. Muscle Head gave the Saxon DJs such clarity on the mic; it really helped bring their lyrics to prominence. He also mixed them down precise and tight – tighter than a homeboy's cornrow.

Another Saxon selector that displayed genius when playing music and mixing down the DJs was Trevor Sax. His approach was different to that of Muscle Head, but he was equally effective.

Trevor's husky voice and short, catchy lyrics all added to the general entertainment, and boosted his high-energy music set. At this stage, we were still enjoying life as freelance DJs. Sometimes we would be chatting on Sir Coxsone or Front Line in Brixton, and then another time we would be back on Buchanan sound in Stockwell. More than likely though, we would be chatting on Saxon in Lewisham.

One day Dennis Rowe rang Smiley and said that he and Muscle Head would like to meet with us. We met with them outside Dennis' house in Lewisham and they expressed concern about a dispute with their regular DJs, Papa Levi and Peter King. Dennis and Muscle Head were determined to secure our full services on Saxon and made us a variety of offers. I'm not joking when I say we were outside the house for hours until Smiley and I finally agreed to give it a go and chat on Saxon permanently.

This was a big step for us because when we spoke about it afterwards we both admitted to feeling somewhat anxious about being tied to just one sound and it wasn't Buchanan. Nevertheless, we had already agreed to the challenge and were prepared to go for it.

The next performance was in Cricklewood, North London and Saxon was the only sound playing. A recording of that event is still out there somewhere, as are many of the tapes from those days. There were only three of us DJing that night – myself, Smiley and Daddy Colonel. Muscle Head got things rolling and as we gathered around the sound, getting ready to take up the mic, the crowd swarmed towards us. Smiley then rocked the house with one of his legendary introductions...

"If you sleep pon you back you bound have fi snore.

Dem de time deh, you spirit walk through the door.

If it don't come back, me say you snore no more.

'Cos death is a ting I say no doctor can cure..."

The three of us received great responses from the crowd. Muscle Head, who never really got too excited about anything, looked at us and repeatedly snarled, "Draw the fast style, draw the fast style..." Daddy Colonel went first, then me and finally Smiley, all drawing our fast styles one after the other as the crowd went wild. Their appreciation lasted right through until the dance finished. We were feeling good about the night; said our "Laters" to Colonel, Muscle Head, D Rowe and the sound crew, and made our way down the stairs towards the exit. To our amazement, on the staircase we saw two boys impersonating us while trying to check two girls. Smiley and I found this so funny, it brought us back to the days when we impersonated U Brown and Nicodemus to chat up girls.

We performed for Saxon at a few more dances and news that we were smashing up the place reached Papa Levi and Peter King, who returned to the fold soon after that. Levi was cheeky, mischievous and could be merciless on the mic. Anyone was fair game when the mood took him. We had to make sure that he understood not to play with us on the mic because we were cultural DJs.

If you listen through the Saxon archives you'll find that Papa Levi certainly respected our request as he never dissed or joked with us on the mic.

Saxon started to mash up dances all over London and even though we were not recording and releasing music, the crowds were singing back our lyrics and giving us big encores as if we were singing well known pop tunes. In Shepherd's Bush one time Levi chanted on the mic just the words, "Born as a chanter..." and the crowd went crazy as if they already knew it. Levi reacted by directly asking the crowd, "Wait, wait, you hear this before?" In North London, the crowd only needed to hear the line "Me know everything 'bout the car..." before going crazy and in East London it was the same for Smiley when he chanted just the words "Anything me chat is roots reality..." This audience response was surprising to us, and especially when you consider that Saxon had no airplay or TV exposure. Also, this was a long time before YouTube or even the Internet's existence. We learnt that such reactions didn't manifest through chance, but were generated through clever marketing and hard work by Dennis Rowe and those around him.

He and his team sat in his house for hours upon hours recording tape after tape so he could distribute them nationally to promote Saxon. He then drove all over London and gave the tapes to people for free so he could create immediate awareness. That was our version of social media back then, and it worked. Tapes took a long time to copy and had to be handled with care – especially the original copies, which got used quite frequently. We can only imagine the kind of effort Dennis and Muscle Head put in to make things develop so quickly.

Muscle Head bought a 7 series BMW and would act as chauffeur to the DJs for dances that were some distance away. At a dance in North London, Smiley, Papa Levi and I felt so big when we got out of the BMW and everyone was watching us as if we were superstars.

We were on such a vibe that the energy we generated in that dance even caused the crowd to boo the home sound and insist they turn off so that Saxon could play right to the end. Saxon's house dances – especially the ones held in Lewisham – were so packed that we had to start going through extreme measures just to get in.

On one occasion we had to be pulled up through the first floor window of a house because the packed crowd made it impossible for us to get in through the front door.

Saxon's popularity was growing rapidly and it gained even more pace when Tippa Irie joined the fold. Tippa brought a fresh, bouncy and melodic energy to Saxon's arsenal of lyrics and the scene was now set for Saxon to take England by storm. Saxon's philosophy was to play *against* other sounds, never with them, and Papa Levi was the key for this as he did not hesitate to diss and bury a sound and their DJs. Levi was fearless, and didn't have a care. On the mic it was total war and if Saxon wasn't playing another sound, then he would turn his attention to the other Saxon DJs. Numerous times Smiley and I laughed at Levi's humour, but I have to admit that on occasions, even we felt embarrassed for people that Levi cussed on the mic. Tippa was dangerous too and he would light bonfires under sounds and their DJs with his mesmerising style.

The noise levels at Saxon dances were legendary, and it was coming from the crowds.

Wherever we went, it reached some serious decibels and most of the time you couldn't hear yourself when you were chatting on the mic for all the whistles, shouting, screaming, stamping, banging and foghorns that were a part of every Saxon dance. Peter King's influence could be heard everywhere as nearly every DJ on every sound system had a fast style now. The only real downside was that everyone else was getting the plaudits for it except for the originator himself, Peter King. He eventually stopped travelling with the sound but his fast style lived on. Everywhere Saxon went, the crowds would demand to hear it and they always went crazy when we obliged.

The competition between DJs to come with fast styles was immense, and so we decided to combine a fast style between the two of us. Smiley was adamant that we had to be credited with creating this style as a combo, and to make sure we include a line that let people know it had never been done before.

We first performed our combined fast style at Lewisham Boys Club when Saxon was playing against two other sounds, one of them being Jamdown Rockers with Champion as their lead DJ.

When we performed it the crowd went so crazy that we had to repeat it about five times! This was how it went...

Asher: "It's I, Asher."

Smiley: "It's I, Smiley."

Asher: "We praise Jah Jah."

Smiley: "The Almighty."

Asher: "Fa dem style yah."

Smiley: "Dem don't easy."

Asher and Smiley: "Never been chat by two MCs."

Asher: "We inna degree."

Smiley: "Past category."

Asher and Smiley: "We chat we lyrics intelligently."

Asher and Smiley: "From January to December, from December to January..."

Our fast style combination caused disbelief amongst the fans. People were even saying that there was no way the two of us were chatting. They were convinced that only one of us had delivered those lyrics. However, when the tape was circulated, people were able to identify our different voices. At this same event in Lewisham Boys Club we realised that Tippa Irie wasn't chatting on the mic and Smiley didn't hesitate to ask him why.

Tippa said that Champion had told him he'd better not chat on the mic tonight for his own good. Smiley told him that no one can stop him from chatting on the mic and that we'd got his back, which inspired Tippa to go straight back onto the mic.

We'd formed a bond with Saxon, and were like family. Every one of us received accolades from fans – not only for ourselves, but for the other DJs too. We found that girls were excited by the Saxon movement just as much as boys, and some of them followed the sound near and far. Later it was brought to my attention that many girls had pictures of Saxon members up on their bedroom walls. London was swinging for us but it was another level up in the countryside - yes, countryside, that's anywhere outside London that you travel to by car, including places like Leicester.

Saxon was being booked all over England and we went to nearly all of the gigs at that time. Sometimes Smiley or I would drive on the country journeys but occasionally we opted to jump in someone else's car. We might see some friends, tell them to jump in the car and surprise them by taking them all the way to a show in the country.

Other times we jumped in friend's cars and encouraged them to drive us to Birmingham, Leicester, Leeds, Manchester or wherever the show may have been. As a matter of fact everyone we took to a show said how much they'd enjoyed the experience, and would always ask to be taken again.

When Smiley got in that driver's seat and we headed for country, one thing you could guarantee was speed. I drove fast but Smiley drove 'fastest', and most times as fast as the car could go. One night we were on the M1 heading north with Smiley at the wheel. We were driving 'fastest' along the part of the M1 that had floodlighting and we didn't realise that we only had our sidelights on. When the motorway lighting suddenly stopped, everything went pitch black. We were initially driving in the fast lane but by the time Smiley had turned on the headlights we were shocked to see that we were now in the slow lane. It was a real adrenaline rush but please don't try it at home... We didn't even learn routes properly. All we had to do was hear which part of the country the show was and we just headed there.

Coming back from a trip in the countryside was rarely straightforward either.

One time there was an entourage of cars all heading back to London and Smiley said, "Let's show them some speed." When he kicked down we left them far behind. To our amazement, when we looked back we saw them turning off the motorway. It was too late for us to turn back by then, so we had to keep on driving for ages until we finally saw a sign that said, "Welcome to Wales…" Dooh. No matter how far the dances were, we always seemed to set off on the journey late and this soon developed into a pattern. It became a habit. It wasn't planned it's just how it went, even though sometimes it wasn't by our design. One night, while we were chilling at Smiley's house in Streatham someone came to check us and showed us a flier with our names on it. It was advertising a Saxon dance in Manchester that was taking place that same night. For whatever reason, we hadn't been informed of this dance and so after some serious deliberation, we decided to go. We had never been to Manchester before and just drove straight up the M1 believing it would lead us to Manchester. It wasn't until we saw signs to Scotland that we realised the M1 doesn't go straight to Manchester!!! Dooh. Anyhow when we finally got to the club, the rave was finished.

The empty beer bottles and drink cans that littered the floor attested to the fact that the dance had been ram-packed. Smiley told Dennis Rowe not to leave yet while we went and found the promoter. We explained to him that we hadn't known about the dance, and described the mix up we'd had getting there. The promoter said in his Manchestonian accent "You should know how to get to Manchester man!" He opened a sports bag full of cash, took out some notes and paid us for our troubles. We then went to Dennis and he also paid us for the inconvenience!

Dennis and Muscle Head worked hard to ensure that everything to do with Saxon was usually structured and well organised. One of our favourite things was to chill out at Dennis Rowe's house in Lewisham. He was really creative, and full of ideas. Like most innovators, some of his ideas were way out there or loopy, whilst others were golden and definitely hit the spot. Whilst talking to Smiley one day, he made reference to a track by the popular Jamaican reggae artist Johnny Ringo that went, "Jamaicans holler rewind, Yankees say replay. Yankees take vacations, we go on holiday. Yankees take dictation, we write essay".

Dennis suggested that Smiley make a cut of it but instead of referring to American and Jamaican, he should do a lyrical interpretation comparing English and Jamaican. It was one of D. Rowe's more on-point ideas and so Smiley began to write 'Cockney Translation.' Funnily enough my sister, who now lives in my mum's house, was cleaning out the basement and found one of my old lyrics books. When I looked through it I was amazed to see Smiley's handwriting and the first fifteen or so lines of 'Cockney Translation.'

"It's I Smiley Culture wid the mic in a me hand.
Me come fi teach you right and not the wrong in a de cockney translation.
Cockney's not a language it is only a slang.
And was originated ya' so in a England.
The first place it was used was over East London.
It was respected for the different style pronunciation.
But it wasn't really used by any and any man.
Me say strictly conman, also the villain but through me full up a lyrics and education, right now you a go get a little translation.
Cockneys have names like Terry, Arthur and Dell Boy.

We have names like Winston, Lloyd and Leroy.

We ball out 'Yow!' while cockneys say 'Oi!'

What cockney call a jacks, we call a blue boy.

Cockney have mates while we have spar.

Cockney live in a drum, while we live in a yard.

We get nyam, while Cockney get capture.

Cockney say governor, we say big bout yah.

In a de cockney translation..."

Once Smiley had learned 'Cockney Translation' he began to perform it in the dances and every time he mimicked the cockney accent the crowd would erupt. He had brought a new element to our continuous rhyming style, and knew that he had to do more with the cockney accent. He said that when I wrote 'Traffic Warden,' this inspired him to write 'Police Officer'. As per usual, he performed it at dances and again, he received tremendous crowd responses when he switched into the cockney accent...

"Well, well. What's your name then son?

'Me name Smiley Culture.'

Where do you think your coming from lad?

'From seeing my mother.'

What you got in the boot then son?

'A cassette recorder, would you like to have a look?'

Shut your bloody mouth! We ask, you answer, now take the keys out of the car and step out of the motor. Me and my colleagues have got a few questions to ask yah.

You'll be on your way as soon as we get an answer..."

I started to work some different accents into my own lyrics, like in the track 'Asher In Court,' where I impersonate a judge's posh tone... "Mr Senator, when you're in a courthouse please remove your beaver..."

By now, it wasn't just our fast styles or continuous rhyming styles that the crowd were going ecstatic for, but also the way we were manipulating accents. We impersonated Americans, Africans, children and even old ladies in our quest to take the DJ thing to higher heights. Even Papa Levi admitted that he was in awe of our lyrical qualities, and he mentioned this on the mic on numerous occasions. When he was clashing at Lewisham Boys Club on 21st October 1983 against Leslie Lyrics he said to Leslie live on the mic, "How you mean Asher don't have no lyrics? As a matter of fact, you think anybody have lyrics like Asher and Smiley?"

The entire club erupted at that, including us. This clash was billed as Papa Levi versus Leslie Lyrics and it was decided that the beginning of the dance would feature me chatting on Saxon, and Dirty Desi chatting on Ghetto Tone, which was the same sound Leslie Lyrics was representing. This clash is historic, and it remains one of the most popular Saxon cassette tapes to this day. It had a personal undercurrent because Leslie Lyrics and his DJ partner Dirty Desi started out on Saxon before breaking away to start Ghetto Tone.

Dennis Rowe repeatedly warned me how Desi had written and prepared battle lyrics for me, and so I was obliged to write a few of my own. When I eventually chatted my battle lyrics it sent the crowd wild, as they were gunning for a lyrical battle. Leslie wasn't impressed with the lyrics I'd attacked Desi with and so when he started his segment in the clash he made reference to me, saying that my lyrics were like a politician's, and how I couldn't step in Desi's shoes. It was this that caused the reaction from Papa Levi who totally defended me. In fact Levi resented Leslie's statement so much that he went even further and demanded respect for Smiley too!

Papa Levi cussed so much in the clash that when we played the tape in the cab office on Wandsworth Road, two men with daring reputations called Jimmy and Fingers kept rewinding Levi's more derogatory lyrics so they could use them when intimidating people. They cheered every "bad man" sentence that Levi said. Levi won the clash but what's bizarre is that at a later date, when Saxon was playing in Peckham, Leslie Lyrics paid Levi back. Leslie had done intensive research into where the actual lyrics were originating from at Saxon and realised that most of the styles were coming from Smiley and myself. Leslie's lyrics that night went something like this...

"Levi clasped his hands and go down pon the floor. And say now we done with '83 and move into '84, he can pirate Smiley and Asher some more..."

Levi was inspired by us just like we were inspired by him, but he wrote his own lyrics and they were among the best of the best. Levi's outward personality on the mic brought him immediate attention, but it left him open for attack from other DJs. Just like the fastest gun in the west there was a bounty on his head, and every DJ wanted him dead or alive.

Sometimes DJs from other sound systems who we'd never heard of before would make plans for him by writing lyrics dissing him directly. One night when some unknown DJ went on the opposing sound's mic and chatted burial lyrics about Levi, it left him begging for someone to tell him the other DJ's name, so he could strike back. The DJ disappeared into the night and was never heard of again. Smiley and I never entertained the battling side of DJing, but continued to rain down cultural and story-time lyrics.

The things we said may have been threatening sometimes and may even have got you thinking, 'What did they mean by that?' but our main focus was to chat sophisticated and uplifting lyrics. Fans labelled us as "intelligent DJs" due to the fact that our lyrics were based on an extensive vocabulary. People approached us before and after dances to ask us to chat lyrics for them and most of the time we felt so indebted to our fans that we happily obliged.

A lot of UK DJs were trying to chat and sound like Josey Wales around this time. He was a celebrated Jamaican DJ, but the Saxon DJs had already developed their own artistic identities and so we didn't follow this trend.

Saxon Invasion 1983

One night Saxon played Unity sound-system in Broadwater Farm, and I opened with lyrics that went...

"Nuff MC a chat like Josey.

Some a dem sound fooly.

Nuff MC a chat like Josey.

What happen to Papa Briggy?

In 1982 it was strictly Briggy.

But now a '83, a just Josey you see.

But we search over land and we search over sea.

We search in de hills and down the gully.

We search in a de town and in the city.

We search in a de alley and round the valley.

But we coulda never find another MC like we.

'Cos through we - eh - nuff chat originally."

Levi was next with lyrics like 'Me Perfect,' then Smiley took the mic and chatted...

"Me born, me raise sey in the ghetto.

As a youth me was wild, but as a man me's a pro.

The Bible say what you reap you will sow."

Another memorable dance was when Saxon played in the Nottingham Palais. When we arrived we spoke to a few locals who said they didn't recognise our names but when we told them which lyrical styles were ours they knew the lyrics instantly and jumped for joy at the prospect that we would be entertaining them later.

By now, Rusty and Sandy had joined Saxon and so when the show started the Nottingham people were getting the full package of what London had been going crazy for. Smiley and I chilled for most of the night, taking in the great entertainment the Saxon DJs were dishing out with lyrics after lyrics. The whistles and the noise element was totally loud right through the night until around 5 am, when it seemed that tiredness had started to sneak in on the crowd and even the DJs. That's when we took hold of the mic and we chatted lyrics until the dance finished well after 7 am.

All the lyrics we chatted that night were based from a cultural perspective and apart from when Levi blessed the tape with 'Mi God Mi King', it was just Smiley and I right through. At one point Smiley bussed lyrics like...

"You see Jah Jah. You see Jah Jah.

Him a fi me Fada-da.

Me know what's to know 'bout fi me Fada-da.

In case you never know Him, ah the Earth's Creator-tor

Sey controlling from before man was ev-ver.

Sey me read up me Bible everyday a chapter-ter.

From Genesis to Kings, from Kings to Isiah-iah.

When me reach Revelation sey me start all over-ver.

Meditate and appreciate the work of Jehovah-vah..."

The plaudits we received from that one dance in particular went on for years. It was circulated among the Saxon posse first and then by the fans and for some reason I recall it being the most requested and talked about live sound-system tape that Smiley and I had ever recorded. People mentioned the spiritual essence of the tape and would enquire how we were so lyrically cultural. Smiley was like me in regards to respecting the Rastafarian culture and most of our early teaching came from their philosophies and values. It was a humble Ras called Chancey that first told us about the forthcoming barcodes and made it sink in by grabbing the Rizla packet and stating "Even the Rizla a go have barcode youth man!"

Rastafari's teachings were heartfelt and we were more than happy relaying the Rastafari message of peace, love and awareness to the people through our lyrics.

Saxon's marketing plans were effective and they were soon booked out seven nights a week all over the UK. We all sensed that we were on the verge of something great. We could feel the wheel of life turning our way and this was reflected in the DJs increasingly opulent lyrics. "Is it really happening to me, mi taking airplane like it a taxi?" asked Tippa Irie, whilst Daddy Colonel announced that, "Saxon done with the struggling, done with the suffering, now for the earning."

Papa Levi hadn't lost sight of what had brought us all this far, and came with the line, "The pile of lyrics sitting in my room are more precious than the gold in Cleopatra's tomb." It would only be a matter of time before he signed to a record label, and we dreamt of the same. The enquiries from people began to come in thick and fast.

Everyone wanted to know when we were going to record our music and it would become a reality soon enough.

Chapter 6

Crossover Hits And Misses

From its inception, reggae music has captured the ears of white owned British record labels. In 1964 a teenage girl from Clarendon, Jamaica had a global hit with a catchy tune called 'My Boy Lollipop'. It was this song that introduced "Blue Beat" or "ska" to the world. Millie was talent spotted by white Jamaican businessman Chris Blackwell, who flew her to South London and launched the iconic Island Records on the back of their hit record. A few years later Island Records signed the original Wailers – Bunny Livingston, Peter McIntosh and Robert Marley, to a two-album deal that brought reggae international exposure. Chris repackaged the group, re-named them Bob Marley and the Wailers and the rest is history.

Another young entrepreneur who took an interest in this new beat from the streets of Jamaica was Richard Branson of Virgin Records. He took a team of his top A & R people to Kingston and signed up many of reggae's early DJ pioneers like U Roy, Tappa Zukie and Althea & Donna for his Frontline label.

It was a ram-packed night at the People's Club in Paddington, and Smiley was on the mic for Saxon. He was receiving a tremendous reception from the crowd.

Smiley performed lyrics after lyrics, two of them being 'Cockney Translation' and 'Police Officer.' John McGillivray, the proprietor of Dub Vendor record shop in Clapham Junction and his business partner Chris Lane, who managed Fashion Records were in attendance that night. After witnessing the crowd's reaction to Smiley's performance they made him an offer to record his music, and for some reason we took it a bit more seriously this time. We'd had invitations to record from different people before but nothing of any great significance.

The next day when Smiley and I linked up, we spoke about this offer for him to record his music. Smiley appreciated the fact that it was a real opportunity for him to become a recording artist but he was even more determined to ensure that I joined him on the journey. He convinced me that we should both sign for the same company and insisted he couldn't do it without me. I was okay with whatever but wasn't sure if Fashion Records would even want to sign me. Smiley demonstrated his loyalty to me and said that he wouldn't sign for Fashion Records unless they signed me too. It was this kind of gesture that separated Smiley from the rest. He was serious and so it proved as time progressed.

Later that same week we went to see John and Chris at Fashion Records in Clapham Junction. Fashion had taken over the basement of Dub Vendor record shop. There were two rooms, one for the actual recording and one live room, and it had a small voicing booth that was originally a toilet. Although this basement was small and compact, it appeared massive and full of promise to us. The record shop was on ground level and on the first floor there was an office that was used as administration for both Dub Vendor and Fashion Records. Papa Face, who was a DJ on Brixton sound Mafia Black, was the main salesman in the record shop while a lovely lady called Cynthia (bless her soul) managed the office.

Chris possessed skills as a musician and was the music producer while John mainly concentrated on the business side of things. John would get involved in the production side by offering some good ideas but his input was more as an executive producer. We came from a sound system background and so this was the first time we'd had any interactions with any record label, let alone one that was white owned. This wasn't a hindrance though, as Chris and John truly loved West Indian culture and reggae music.

During Smiley's first meeting with them they praised him and showered him with appreciation for the 'Cockney Translation' lyrics he'd chatted at the People's Club and offered to sign him on a one-year contract. Smiley being Smiley informed them that he was grateful for their offer but would only sign to Fashion Records if they also signed me. It was a no brainer for Chris and John, so they agreed. We returned at a later date to collect the recording and publishing contracts they'd had prepared and were advised by Chris and John to take them to a solicitor so that we understood the terms clearly. I hope our next actions may serve as a lesson to some of you younger readers so if you find yourself in a similar situation at any time in your personal careers, please remember it and use our mistake as a pointer of what *not* to do.

The road that leads to hell is full of big intentions and small miscalculations. We were so excited by the prospect of a recording deal and so eager to get things moving that we never took the contracts to solicitors at all. We just pretended to John and Chris that we had. Yes, we read them through and got our own understanding of what was in them but realistically we were novices in regards to contract law.

We read and were aware that the recording contract offered 6% for the artist and the publishing contract offered a 50% split between the artist and Fashion Records. That sounded good, real good, and it still felt good for about three months until we received our first royalty and publishing payments.

When it came closer to the time for us to sign the contracts Smiley became concerned about how the reggae dancehall crowd would perceive him for doing the cockney accent. He had reservations and was worried that they would class him as a sell-out. I had to remind him about the massive appreciation that he was already receiving, not just for 'Cockney Translation' but also for a multitude of his lyrics. So we signed the recording and publishing contracts and began recording our first tracks.

This was a new experience for us and initially we found it a challenge having to adjust our chatting styles from chatting in the dancehall to recording in a studio. Chris was serious and demanded professionally recorded tracks with no corners cut so we had to work hard on things like our timing, tone and lyrical structures.

He let us know from early on that we needed to have choruses so that people could sing along and the choruses needed to drop at specific points in the track, after every eight bars. So we spent time adding choruses to our lengthy lyrics and since Chris was adamant that we recorded with as few drop-ins as possible, this meant we practiced hard.

"Drop-ins" occur when an artist stops during a recording and then instead of starting over, they continue recording from where they left off. Chris made sure our tracks had as few drop-ins as possible since they disturbed the flow of the lyrics on the track. As time went on we understood and respected where he was coming from and even started to identify drop-ins that were used in other DJs' tracks. He had us back and forth from home to the studio telling us to come back tomorrow when we had the lyrics tighter.

After a while we became expectant of a "go back home and rehearse" demand from Chris until one day when Smiley had finished voicing 'Cockney Translation' and come out of the voicing booth Chris yelled, "That's the one!" and finally we felt the ball begin to roll.

It was now just a matter of time before 'Cockney Translation' would be released on Fashion Records and the anticipation was immense. Fashion Records had already produced a national hit by Laurel and Hardy called 'Clunk Click'. It had caught people's imaginations since it highlighted police harassment and their actions when putting people in the back of their vans. "Clunk Click, you're nicked..."

Whilst waiting for 'Cockney Translation' to be released we attended a house dance in Notre Dame Estate in Clapham Common and witnessed a major turning point in the UK DJ history. I've already mentioned that Papa Levi had recorded a track produced by Maxi Priest and Barry Boom but we could not, would never have expected or even imagined what we heard and saw that night. When the sound system played Papa Levi's track 'Mi God Mi King' the crowd went mad right from the start so the operator pulled it up and played it again. Man, the crowd went mad for the track at least three times and it had not even got to the part where he performed the fast style yet. When the track did get to the fast style part the crowd went berserk. It was amazing.

154

All we could say was 'Raaaaaaaaaa' and wish for the day when Smiley's single 'Cockney Translation' and my first track 'Abbreviation Qualification' are released.

Then 'BOOM!' 'Cockney Translation' was released and it flew to No. 1 in the UK reggae charts. Promoters started to book us to perform on stage at events all over England. These personal appearances or "PAs" contractually consisted of a three-track performance but we often did more because of the crowd's demands, and all of those passionate shouts of "Forward!" Militant Mikey was our selector at these PAs. He knew most of our lyrics off by heart and this helped him to master mixing the beat for us when we performed. Sometimes when we forgot a line on stage Mikey would shout out the lyrics and get us back on track. PA shows were coming in thick and fast and when Channel 4 contacted Fashion Records to see if they could film us performing, we agreed to do a show at the One O Club in Catford. This show featured Papa Face, Bionic Rhona, Maxi Priest, Asher Senator and Smiley Culture and as per usual, it was ram-jammed. The crowd were stamping on the floors and banging on the walls in the club with such enthusiasm that bits were falling off the walls and roof.

We literally mashed the place down. When Smiley performed 'Cockney Translation,' the crowd sang along with it word for word. It was so overwhelming that Smiley had to stop the music and plead with the crowd to share the lyrics! Nights like those kept our heads buzzing and I remember watching it back on Channel 4 feeling 'Wow'. Click on thumbs up when you watch this dance on YouTube, seen?

'Abbreviation Qualification' flew to No. 2 on the UK Reggae Charts and also caused a storm on 12". It was a double A side. On the flipside was 'Fast Style Origination' which describes the origin and development of the fast style. Smiley and I always spoke about Peter King the fast style originator and how he just disappeared off the scene. We certainly didn't like how so many people were getting credit for what he'd done and that was the main reason why I was inspired to write 'Fast Style Origination.' Smiley suggested that we should go to see him and offer him the chance to record on Fashion Records with us. When we met up with him, we got on well straight away and began to write and vibes lyrics together. We encouraged him to become involved again and soon he became part of the team.

Peter King taught us all the driving short cuts from Lewisham to Brixton as we were always moving between each other's areas. Smiley loved Peter King, just like I did but we soon found out that this guy was... let's just say different in his thinking and actions. He later proved he was a man who did whatever he had to do in certain situations, without remorse.

Smiley could also switch in a heartbeat, like when the joy of receiving his first royalty statement shifted quickly to pain. When he saw his statement for one thousand odd pounds after selling over ten thousand copies of 'Cockney Translation,' he said, "This just can't work" and I felt the same after selling over five thousand copies of 'Abbreviation Qualification' and receiving a royalty statement of around £500. The surprisingly low payments we received were due to our naivety and our unprofessional attitudes towards signing contracts without consulting a solicitor.

Smiley was always speaking to me about our worth. He saw the bigger picture from early and never stopped painting it for me to see. His picture contained stardom and money to back it up, which was justified in my eyes because of the attention our music was generating.

We went to visit John and Chris at Dub Vendor and after expressing our concerns with regards to the royalties, Smiley asked them to increase the royalty percentage on his next track 'Police Officer' which was due to be released soon. After long and hard negotiations John and Chris eventually agreed to this, and they also agreed to increase our publishing percentages from 50% to 60% in our favour. It was just a verbal agreement but the results from the negotiations pleased us and we used some of the monies from our first royalty payments quite wisely.

I took £100 from mine and bought a 4-track recording machine while Smiley used a considerable amount of his to equip and build a small, but professional recording studio in his mother's flat in Lansdowne Green Estate. After a while he started to invite local young artists to the studio and gave them the opportunity to record their songs and lyrics. He recorded Mannix, whose voice was so smooth that every girl who heard him sing testified to how sexy it was. Also Stewie Love, who earned the title "Mellow Canary" since he was able to hit the high singing notes that are usually associated with female singers.

Mannix recorded a memorable soul song called 'Your Love' while Stewie recorded a reggae song called 'You Told Me You'd Be Saving Your Love'. They were just two of the local talents who enjoyed the benefits of Smiley's little studio. He recorded a few others but he was very particular about who was allowed into his studio. He certainly wasn't allowing any riff-raff to come in to unsettle a family set up, so he made sure people were vetted from afar. Sometimes he'd ban someone from the studio without them knowing and it's funny because Smiley installed himself as judge and jury and if he found them guilty by reputation they were banned for life, with no appeal. We had learnt so much from Chris of Fashion Records when it came to professionally recording music and vocals and passed this on to the artists we worked with.

Nothing had changed when Smiley had to voice his second track 'Police Officer' since Chris continued from where he left off with his usual "no nonsense" approach to recording vocals. Every time Smiley finished what we thought was the completed vocal Chris would tell him to re-voice it and after a few hours of that he'd then send Smiley home to practice.

To voice 'Police Officer' was becoming a task and just as I was when voicing my tracks, Smiley became agitated by the amount of hoops he had to jump through. It was our hard upbringing in the DJ business that helped us to accept this as just another challenge and so Smiley practiced long and hard until he'd perfected the vocal style for 'Police Officer.' Believe me, it was a relief for us all when Chris finally gave 'Police Officer' the all clear and I actually remember us celebrating as if we'd just scored the winning goal in the last seconds of the FA cup. When they played the track, everyone in the studio acknowledged that there was something special about 'Police Officer', but to be quite honest Smiley and I thought all of our lyrics were special and so to us it was just another showstopper. 'Police Officer' was now ready to be played to visitors who would pass through Fashion Records. When they played Muscle Head the track all he said after listening to it all the way through was "Number 1," and Capital Radio DJ and reggae aficionado David Rodigan agreed with him.

Smiley and I were still performing PAs when 'B-O-O-M!!!!!' 'Police Officer' went to No. 1 in the UK Reggae Charts and then 'B-O-O-M!!!!!' it was at No. 12 in the UK national pop charts.

Smiley was now the UK's biggest reggae artist and the whole world was waiting for him. It was a real change to all those nights bashing out lyrics on Smiley's Marantz stereo. He was now a real superstar and entitled to bask in his moment of glory, and Smiley loved every minute of it. Mikey, Fox, King and I caught a little of the stardust as well as Smiley received awards left, right and centre.

Long before the MOBOs, the first reggae awards were hosted by DJ Tony Williams, who had a show on Radio London. That night Smiley cleaned up and won three awards. He won 'Best British Reggae Record', 'Best Newcomer' and 'Most Record Sales'. He collected his awards with dignity but immediately after the event when we'd climbed into his car, his true emotions took over. He broke down in tears and triggered a crying reaction throughout the car as Mikey, Fox, King and I joined in. It was a moment to cherish and certainly one of the special occasions that brought us even closer as a family unit.

Everyone was feeling the track 'Police Officer' by this time – even the police. Smiley signed so many autographs for the Metropolitan Police he could have been their cheque bearer. It's strange thinking about that now.

We were returning from a concert in the country one night, and I was driving a little fast as we passed by the roundabout at the beginning of Old Kent Road. A police van full of police stopped us and asked me, the driver, to get out of the car. Smiley jumped out at the same time and said "Officer, don't you know who I am?" The officer recognised him and called the other police officers out of the van. They even brought out their 'Police Officer' records and asked him to sign them. The police left happily but on their way back to the van turned to me and said, "Slow down mate". On numerous other occasions, once the police saw that Smiley Culture was with us they didn't want to see any driving documentation at all. Life imitated music. It was as if the Metropolitan Police had been sent a memo not to give Smiley a producer, until we were driving through North London one night with Smiley at the wheel. Two police officers pulled us over and the first thing Smiley said when he got out of the car was "Officer, do you know who I am?" The officer just looked at him and replied, "NO, BUT WE'RE GONNA FIND OUT TONIGHT". This was a no nonsense officer – one who was most likely on leave when they sent out the memo, and he was backed up by a colleague who was equally determined to secure an arrest.

We had weed on us so it was becoming mightily tense as this police officer began to delve a little deeper with his forensic questioning. It eventually took a fight breaking out across the road between a man and his woman before the police abandoned us to deal with that instead, shouting for us to "stay there and don't move until we get back". Yeah right! Smiley just handed them one of his business cards, said "Call me" and we drove off. They were so pissed.

Smiley couldn't hide his delight as 'Police Officer' swept across England like a tsunami. Since I'd changed my name to Senator, Smiley had become accustomed to calling me Seny and when Top Of The Pops came knocking I recall him saying "Seny this is unbelievable, TOP OF THE POPS man!" He said that his heart rate had accelerated from the time they told him about Top Of The Pops and he didn't know if it would ever slow down again. BBC's Top Of The Pops was the No. 1 music show on British TV. In fact at one stage I'm sure it was the only music show on TV. When 'Police Officer' hit it had 18 million viewers a week, so for Smiley to be performing on there was extraordinary.

All of the big superstars performed on Top Of The Pops, as it was the one chart that the music industry and its consumers relied on for indication of the highest selling records. That moment was surreal and even I was in awe. Smiley kept me so close to the situation that it felt as if it was me performing, so I can only imagine the sensation he felt. We discussed how he should dress for Top Of The Pops, and at the end of the day decided that he would wear a full white suit, which turned out to be a choice of genius. All eyes were on him and his performance propelled the track up the charts. The UK DJ movement was now stampeding through record companies and the media. Smiley was performing at national clubs up and down the country whilst making sure that the team was always there, and that I was mostly performing alongside him. Those were exciting times to be a reggae DJ, coming from humble beginnings on homemade sound systems to making records, and the labels soon came calling. Greensleeves Records signed up most of the Saxon DJs for their UK Bubblers label, Maxi Priest signed a deal with Virgin and Papa Levi signed a contract with Chris Blackwell's Island Records. Not to put too fine a point on it, but we all got weighed out.

With the success of 'Police Officer,' newspaper and magazine interviews were now standard procedure for Smiley and I think he must have been featured in every paper and magazine possible. Fashion hired a publicist by the name of Alan Edwards and he did such a good job that Smiley Culture became a household name very quickly.

Most of us kept up-to-speed with what other DJs were saying in their newspaper interviews and Smiley was disappointed with a Tippa Irie interview that he perceived as disrespect. Tippa had said something along the lines of "Smiley had sold out because he was too commercial". Smiley wasn't happy to say the least and so we drove over to Dennis Rowe's house where he confronted Tippa about it. Tippa said that he didn't mean any harm by what he'd said and the matter was resolved amicably enough. We all got paid after all, but at the time we could not articulate the distinctions between selling out and cashing in.

Show money was rolling in by now which meant Smiley was able to upgrade his car and he also upgraded my car while he was at it. He bought a black coloured Vauxhall Royal for himself and a burgundy coloured Opel Senator for me.

Smiley's royalty cheques were exactly the same size as mine, it's just that his had a few more zeros on them, so he took action to ensure that his sparring partner would be fronting in the same style. I was ecstatic with the gift so believe me I wasn't happy when we drove our two cars round to show them to my son's mother Marfier. She lived in Notre Dame Estate and said that Smiley's long, black car looked like a hearse. He wasn't concerned at the comment, or at least that was the impression he gave, but I found it awkward. Marfier couldn't see why I was upset and said it was just a harmless comment but the way I see it, some comments are best kept to ourselves. (Nuff love, Marf). Just like our lyrics, our cars were the talk of the town and especially seeing that we lived in them more than our bedrooms. Whenever we weren't rehearsing or recording we would be driving up and down in them. We'd be driving my car most of the time but Smiley always ensured that it had petrol.

The more popular we became, the more the girls wanted to know. Gone were the days of us impersonating other stars to check girls as the girls were now checking us, and sometimes they chased after us with a passion.

Some girls chased us like in the Beatles film 'A Hard Day's Night,' for real! A live radio show held in Chelsea by Tony Williams underlined the enormity of Smiley's popularity when girls chased us both so hard, the police had to provide protection. We'd arrived to the show late and got in alright but when it was time to leave, it was a whole other story. Loads of girls were camped outside the studio and were waiting for us to come out. We waited for some time but eventually we decided to take a chance and burst through the crowd of girls. We got through but the girls' reaction was to stampede and they rushed after us. Some big superstars complain incessantly about the pressure from fans, but I say at least they have the capacity to employ as many security guards and bouncers as they deem fit. While we ran down this venue's massive staircase, we could hear the screams of the girls behind us. By the time we got outside the building they'd caught up with Smiley and were pulling at him like a rag doll until the police intervened. Another show in Brighton was ridiculously full with white girls and after our performance when we were signing autographs these girls were saying things to us like, "I will do anything for you" and "please take me with you..."

These were proper, professional groupies, no messing, and any place in the vicinity would do. They just wanted to take it to pound town and shag our brains out. We weren't complaining as you can imagine but looking back now, I'd put it down as "experiencing the lessons of life". Smiley and I spoke on numerous occasions about how so many girls only loved us because of our success with music. Some girls told us straight that they didn't want a relationship with us, but just a fling with popularity. How our girlfriends at the time coped was another matter. The arguments that we went through with them over other women were frequent enough, but we had no power over our fans' emotions and some girls even found out where we lived. Man, that was armshouse but what can I say? 'Mad over we and dem a mad over we, boom'.

All those girls certainly kept us on our toes but it was some of our exuberant and never-say-die male friends who made life quite difficult for us on occasions. The beliefs that some of our friends had on how various situations should be handled taught us to think first, and analyse and assess anyone we took with us to shows beforehand.

We were only too aware that any accusations would be followed with the cry, "It was Smiley and Asher dem" and that was irritating to say the least, especially when we had no control over certain situations. We performed at a show in Leeds where for some reason and totally against our standard policy, we had agreed with the promoter to receive our full fee at the end of the show, wrong move. The promoter disappeared just before the end of the show without paying anyone. All of the artists were dismayed but little did we know that one of our friends took on the challenge to find the promoter somewhere in Leeds. Here's a tip, always have someone in your posse who is good at finding stuff. When he returned he was in a real hurry as he said that he'd found the promoter, rushed him and took a bag of money from him. We later found out that he'd actually harmed this guy whilst persuading him to release the cash. Another tip – always have someone in your posse who is prepared to go that extra mile. It was risky to take certain friends with us to shows but on the other hand, it could turn out to be quite handy when they could be used as a form of security. There were some shows where afterwards we agreed that we could have done with a few of our so called harder friends' support.

Like at a Fashion Records show in Leicester for example, where we'd just finished performing to a ram-packed, two thousand strong crowd and introduced the next act, Maxi Priest. As we were leaving the stage, Smiley unwittingly placed the mic at the front of the stage where people in the front row could reach it. When the host of the show went to look for it, it had gone – someone from the audience hadn't been able to resist the temptation and had taken it. The banter between the crowd and the host, who was using another mic, went on for a while as he begged them to give it back since it was the main performance mic. Eventually, after no want of trying the host came up with what seemed like a great idea at the time and announced to the crowd. "People, Maxi Priest was going to use the microphone that has been stolen, so if it is not returned there can be no show. We're going to turn off the light to save the person who took it any embarrassment, and they'll have the chance to put it back anonymously..."

I was standing behind the stage curtains next to Errol Robinson, bless his soul. He was a bass player with the reggae group One Blood but he wasn't well and needed to be connected to an oxygen tank at all times.

When the lights went out I heard a thud and felt someone's body weight fall beside me. When the lights came back on we realised that someone had thrown the mic back and it had hit poor Errol on his head. He was unconscious and backstage was in turmoil so the host went out and addressed the crowd again, saying, "Someone threw the mic and it has injured the bass player, so the show is cancelled..." What! The crowd was not having it and their restlessness turned to rowdiness as they shouted out their disapproval. "This is a con!" "Maxi Priest is not even here!" and "We want our money back!" The threat of physical violence got so great that Maxi Priest went on stage to try and calm things down by reiterating what the host had told them. It was all to no avail and some of the crowd went as far as insisting he was a fake Maxi Priest, and an imposter. Just as I thought things couldn't get any worse, the crowd started to riot. First we stood in amazement as we watched them rushing the two bars for money, and then to our astonishment they stormed the stage to rob the equipment. Smiley and I went into personal survival mode as Chris from Fashion Records began trying to fend off the attackers and shouted for us to assist him in saving his equipment.

We thought, 'Are you mad'? But we went out there for a while and helped push away opportunists until the crowd's persistence became too overpowering. We thought in unison, 'this can't work'. The only option left for us was to retreat and take cover in the dressing rooms, but then the hooligans began kicking at the door as they turned their attention to the artists and musicians. We were completely surrounded, and also overwhelmed by the noise. It was like a scene from the movie Zulu, only set in a club in England. It seemed like only a matter of minutes before the aggressors broke in and we'd be swamped so me, Smiley, Mikey and Fox started to break the legs off some wooden chairs to use for protection. If I remember correctly, Chris was still out there fighting to save his equipment whilst all that was happening. Much to our relief, the banging and kicking at our door finally subsided, the crowd began to disperse and the noise died down. When we emerged from the changing room we saw that the crowd had totally wrecked the venue, robbed both drink bars and got away with some of Chris' equipment.

The important thing was that we'd all survived, and Errol recovered from having been hit by the mic.

That show, out of all the ones we did, was the one where we wished that we'd taken some of our more "up for it" friends with us. The only real problem that lingered on after the show was that Chris kept complaining about how he'd been left on his own to save his equipment. But then after a while he stopped mentioning it, and so I suppose he learned to live with it.

We mainly stuck to our original format of attending shows with just Mikey and Fox accompanying us and the events in Leicester didn't deter us from draping ourselves in gold. Heavy-duty sized gold chains and rings on every finger were our trademark no matter where we performed or travelled to. As far as we were concerned we had this thing locked and the situation that happened in Leicester was just a one-off.

Smiley was on the mic at a ghetto show in Birmingham and there were some locals being somewhat disrespectful with their comments every time the music stopped. While the girls at the front of the small stage and most of the other people in the club were totally enjoying the performance these guys who were hitched in a corner to our right were shouting out things such as, "Play the music and stop talking".

"We run things round here" and "Mind what you're saying". Smiley "fronted" it by sending out requests on the mic to big-shot people who were not even at the show. The names that Smiley mentioned were of famous Jamaican people who were respected around the world for either being top artists or just people that you "behaved" yourself in their presence. This helped the disrespect to stop as the fools believed Smiley, and thought these very popular people must have been somewhere in the club. It was a clever move and we used this same technique at other shows and dances where we found it necessary to calm down the bad boys of that specific area. We understood the dynamics that made some guys a bit jealous because we'd come to their area and were admired by the girls, but it still had to be addressed wisely and peacefully.

Fashion Records was as popular as ever and Dub Vendor was certainly flourishing as it was always filled with reggae head customers. John "Dub Vendor" had his means of ensuring the shop's Jamaican music stock was always current and in some cases, even ahead of the game. This meant that owners of sound systems and their representatives would always make sure they bought their pre-release records from Dub Vendor.

Even we bought our records from Dub Vendor as we piled up our music selections. We would purchase on a trust basis until royalty payday came around, and then we'd reluctantly pay it back. Eventually it came to the time for Smiley to receive his royalty statement for 'Police Officer.' When he looked at his statement and saw the amount he was given for selling over 200,000 records he blew his lid like a pressure cooker that's been left boiling overtime. Fashion Records had not increased the 6% on the contract to 8% as per their verbal agreement and Smiley couldn't believe it. He said that he felt betrayed and dismayed. He'd already made plans for what he was going to do with some of the money but now those plans would be scuppered. The fact of the matter was that it wasn't just Smiley who would feel the loss, because the people he was supporting financially would feel it too. He admitted that the money was one thing, but was passionate in stating that it was also the principle. He said that he had to sort it out with Fashion and aimed to do so with diplomacy except it never quite went according to plan. Smiley went to Dub Vendor and was sitting down in their office on first floor reasoning with John and Chris, who were now denying there was any agreement.

They were saying that they never agreed to a percentage increase and this eventually triggered an angry reaction from Smiley. He grabbed their chunky 1980's style computer and headed towards the window, threatening to throw it out before he smashed up the rest of the place. I jumped on his back shouting, 'No Smiley!' and managed to stop him from going any further with his actions. John and Chris were clearly shook up and said they would pay the increase but after a week or so it became apparent that they weren't going to pay the increase and so it progressed, or should I say digressed to solicitors. They even went as far as walking out of a legal meeting because they didn't like the direction it was taking.

Smiley was due to record his album with Fashion but this was put on hold because of all the negotiations and non-negotiations. He refused to work with Fashion and they put a block on him recording anywhere else, which was sticky as Polydor Records were waiting in the wings to sign him. I was used to him speaking constantly to me about his feelings and plans, and I could see that this situation had affected him deeply.

His emotions were running high amidst the turmoil engulfing his career, and he was truly saddened by the events that were taking place. He'd speak about fairness and even considered leaving things as they were, but deep down he knew he couldn't because he had worked hard for so many years to reach the position he was in. Two hit songs and a bombardment of hits to come from the Cockney Translator meant there was so much promise on the horizon yet he was so frustrated during this period that he sought professional advice from various places. No matter who he consulted, his position remained the same - Smiley was prohibited from recording any music. Some people gave him personal and committed advice but their sentiment did little to expel his disappointment. It was breaking his heart and it showed in his emotions. He still wrote lyrics but they would be semi-finished or simply directed at the situation. He confided his deepest thoughts to me and I felt his anxiety as he complained that the extended delay may affect his career in such a way that it may never recover. The delay continued and seemed to go on forever until eventually Fashion Records withdrew their stance and agreed to pay the increase.

It was late in the day but Smiley appreciated the turn around and immediately made plans to record his album with Polydor. It had taken the best part of a year to reach this point and he couldn't contain his joy when normal play was resumed. Then, just as he thought it was safe to go back into the water, Fashion Records popped up with a "put together" of his recordings, some of them unfinished, and subsequently released them on an album. Smiley's emotions were thrown again and he didn't like it one bit. He didn't like the album at all, and labelled the unfinished material as "rubbish." At one point he looked to me for some kind of deliverance. Again, I felt his hurt but was admittedly lost for any kind of solution. Still, he knew he had my support no matter what. Smiley contacted Fashion Records to let them know of his disappointment and disapproval. He collected his improved royalties for 'Police Officer' and made plans to receive payment for the 'unfinished' album they'd released. The album was called 'The Original Smiley Culture' and featured tracks like 'Police Officer', 'Cockney Translation', 'Slam Bam', 'Shan A Shan', 'Entertainer-Entertainer' and 'Roots Reality' with the lines:

"Anything me chat is roots reality.

And fi ride any riddim, I man have the ability.

Fi mek style, lyrics and tune, fi sit down pon music

continuously.

More time when me feel the vibes, me go in ah it vigorously.

Endlessly, confidently and without no apology.

Now hear me now elders, listen me good now pickney.

Style, lyrics and tune a no one or two things to me, they're

three separately.

And if you don't understand, just listen me properly..."

I was still contracted to Fashion Records and wanted to complete my next album with them. I had already recorded and released a Top 3 single ('Match of The Day"), a No. 1 album ("UK Meets JA") and I was preparing the album 'Born To Chat' which also went on to become successful in the UK reggae album charts. Polydor released Smiley's album called 'Tongue In Cheek' which included tracks like 'School Time Chronicle', 'Mr Kidnapper', 'Customs Officer' and 'Cockney Translator'. The lyrics for 'Cockney Translator' went something like this...

"Me a go cork dis dance yah later 'cos a later will be greater.

Smiley Culture a de Cockney Translator and Senator him a me brother.

Same father, but different mother.

The other day we buck up pon some East Ender.

And dem deh man tuff, dem man no tender.

Threaten fi mix me and Seny in a cement mixer.

But through we a entertainer, they had to reconsider.

Especially when dem find out me a de Cockney Translator.

Cha! Smiley Culture you a de Cockney Translator..."

Those lyrics and many others on that album smashed up many dances and shows although Smiley thought that it could have been done somewhat better. To his credit, that same album was signed on three different occasions to three different record labels. Despite this, the album was never really promoted and so for Smiley to earn at least half a million pounds for it over a period of time showed his knack for turning nothing into something, and something into more.

Chapter 7

A-List VIP

There can be no hiding from the fact that Smiley was never the same artist after his dispute with Fashion Records. Outwardly he was still Smiley Culture, "The Cockney Translator", but something inside him had died. Unfortunately, it was that something which sparked his creative energy.

Did the mainstream media know what we were saying? Did they care? Ethnic representation on British TV was sparse. I remember my family calling out to each other whenever a black person appeared on television... "Come quickly there's a black person on TV!" There were a few newsreaders and presenters who were regular faces. The comedian Lenny Henry was establishing himself. Black footballers and athletes were breaking through, but it was standard for rival supporters to throw bananas at the black players of the opposing team. Well if I look at it lyrically, bananas do contain scientifically proven health benefits...

One of the few black presenters at the time was Trevor Phillips. He presented a show called The London Program for London Weekend Television.

The lack of opportunities for black and Asian people to forge a career in the media was compounded by the fact that there were only three terrestrial TV stations – BBC1, BBC2 and ITV. Landmark shows such as Roots and Empire Road were few and far between. In the early 1980's a new independent, commercial TV station was launched and Channel 4 proved fresh and progressive – especially with its youth culture and ethnic programming. One afternoon, we were kicking back at Smiley's flat in Lansdowne Green Estate when he received a phone call from Trevor Philips. He was ringing to offer Smiley the opportunity to audition as the host of a new music TV series called Club Mix, due to be broadcast soon. Smiley told him straight that he would not audition but Trevor told him that the audition was standard procedure, and he was a strong favourite with the show's production team. He did the audition, was given the part and would host the show for two years. During this time, Smiley was awarded various sponsorships. He wore exquisite suits from Bruce Jeremy and received special invitations to high profile events from very influential people. Artists who were invited onto the show to perform loved Smiley and he formed many friendships.

A-List VIP

The admin team secured performances from global artists and that included our own Maxi Priest. Greats such as Millie Jackson, the late Delroy Wilson, Mary Wilson from Diana Ross' legendary singing group The Supremes and our friends from Saxon sound-system all blessed the Club Mix stage and helped to make it a hit TV show. The Club Mix set was assembled in the style of a regular jazz club with a performance stage set in the middle of the hall; tables and chairs positioned in the middle of the dance floor in front of the stage and standing balconies situated around the sides. A small band made up of three musicians set up at the side of the performance stage and every week they would play original music for Smiley to chat live over and also to cover intermissions. Key people of the show's admin team like Susan and Winsome put in the hard work that was required to make the show a success. They were the engine room; and everything went through them first while at the same time they made it their duty to ensure that Smiley was always excellently catered for. In terms of the show, he would receive a concept for an episode around a day before recording, and have to write and learn a two-minute rap in time to perform it. Most of the time, it was Mikey, Fox and me who contributed lyrics to the two-minute rap.

A-List VIP

Smiley was walking in and out of the LWT studios all the time and so it became standard procedure for us to be there too. He even made it possible for Peter King and I to perform a track called 'Dem Too Lie' on the first series of the show. We dressed in gangster suits for the performance and addressed the lyrics directly to Margaret Thatcher and members of the Conservative cabinet with reference to some of their political lies. Looking back now, I'm surprised they allowed it to be aired in the first place because we rapped about ganja, women and politics in a way that you couldn't get away with today. Did the producers and TV executives really understand what we were saying? Did they care? But this was the new era of alternative comedy; including the satirical TV show Spitting Image.

For the last episode of the show's second series Smiley arranged it so that he and I could perform a combination together. However, on the lead up to the last show he'd threatened to stay off sick and hand in a doctor's certificate because they wanted to sacrifice our performance and replace it with a second song from Maxi Priest. Smiley threw his toys out of the pram and was adamant that he would miss the whole show unless we were allowed to perform our track.

184

The producers had no option but to give in to his diva-like strop. You can see us performing 'Keeping A Dance' on YouTube – remember to "thumbs up" and add it to your playlist...

Club Mix was aired on Channel 4 at around 7 pm on Tuesdays which meant that no matter where we were or what we were doing, if we were in England, we always stopped what we were doing to watch it. I remember us waiting downstairs in a house in North London for Peter King while he entertained a girl upstairs. The room we were in didn't have a television and so when we realised that Club Mix was about to start, we ran upstairs and went into the room where King was in full swing. We said, "Don't mind us", turned the TV over and began to watch Club Mix. King and the girl just carried on right there on the settee next to us as we watched our favourite TV show.

The success of Club Mix kept Smiley's popularity sky-high and no doubt his ego was close behind... maybe even ahead, as it shoved little people out of the way to open more doors. Girls were going crazy out of their heads for Smiley Culture and on a few occasions some disappeared with him into the changing rooms at LWT while he was preparing for filming.

Some even left their boyfriends waiting for some time while Smiley spirited them away to "sign autographs". The sheer aura of Club Mix brought in work for Smiley like the Nat West Bank commercial and in some cases for me too, like the rap for Cilla Black's (bless her soul) TV program Surprise Surprise. Funnily enough, when LWT offered Smiley the chance to do the rap for Cilla Black he accepted even though he had a busy schedule. They took us into a cinema room in LWT and showed us a video of what the rap should be about. After leaving the studios Smiley immediately put it in my hands and said "You write that Seny", so I did. Watching that playback on TV was a fulfilling experience. The two years that Club Mix was broadcast certainly extended our careers. Smiley made many more TV appearances and performances and included me on any of them he could. One thing is for sure – even in later years, he was so proud of this part of his life and he played the videos and spoke about Club Mix frequently; especially around Christmas when he held gatherings for family and friends.

Overall, I can say that we became celebrities even before we became famous. In fact, even before we signed to Fashion Records, people thought that we'd already made it.

And we'd already acquired the exterior trappings of success – the cars, the clothes and the bling. We were celebrities in the community, and receiving acknowledgement and respect was a given. But when 'Cockney Translation' and 'Police Officer' buss, our recognition skyrocketed tenfold, and especially after Smiley debuted on Top of the Pops. Almost overnight we took a quantum leap from street credibility to ghetto superstars; proper VIPs' in the area and beyond. Not that it changed us; as I said people already treated us like we made it. What it did change is the circle of people we connected with, or the people who tried to connect with us. Success, in any shape or form is a strange beast. It attracts all manners of hangers-on and fair-weather friends. We stayed true to our real friends, and they and our families kept us grounded.

Although Smiley Culture's lyrics reflected everyday reality in the black community and his most popular lyrics when chatting on sound systems were roots and culture, his two biggest hits were viewed as rebellious and anti-establishment. The Arthur Daley mock-up record sleeve for 'Cockney Translation' attracted London's gangland fraternity.

Every form of delinquent from plastic hoodlums to genuine, bona fide – "if you look at me the wrong way I'll slice your face off" – gangsters wanted to get to know us. The stop and search and spliff themes of 'Police Officer' directly appealed to young black men – victims of the overzealous manner in which the police would pull up and shakedown any black guy driving a car, even if he was parked up outside a church on a Sunday with a King James Bible clearly resting on the front seat. The musical press hailed us for our innovations, creativity and originality on the microphone. They credited Smiley for his fusion of wit and lyrics that told of life on the streets, as it was.

That's right people, we invented "gangster rap" and the mainstream media – specifically the red tops – became more focused on exposing Smiley's perceived connections to the underworld. Journalists working for some of the nation's top selling newspapers would approach him and make feeble attempts to bait him into giving exclusives on drug dealers, armed robbers and "steaming" gangs. We had our heads screwed on though, and the reporters who tried to entice Smiley were clumsy and naive in their efforts. We were always two steps ahead and far too savvy to fall for their tricks.

We lived by our code, an unwritten, but regimented code that instinctively told us when to keep our mouths shut; when to speak up, and who we could trust with certain information. At that time everyone wanted to interview us from small, self-published magazines to the big hitters like Rolling Stone and NME.

I can't remember the movie, but I remember the feeling, sitting in my cinema seat, popcorn in one hand and Ribena in the next, paying no attention to the slickly produced adverts on the big screen. Then suddenly, I heard Smiley Culture's voice. At first I thought he was sitting somewhere behind me or in front of me, and then he appeared larger than life on the screen – Smiley Culture fronting a million pound advertising campaign for Nat West Bank. I looked around and took in the filmgoers' reactions. At that time TV commercials for major companies and banks were normally the domain of TV actors and film stars. This was Orson Welles' territory. I felt a wave of emotions at that moment.

Mainly, proud of my friend and MC partner, and well pleased and honoured to be associated with someone who had reached this level of achievement.

These were exciting times. When living the dream, everything becomes upgraded then I had an afterthought. 'When will it be my time? When will cinemagoers passively watch me flogging stuff on the big screen while they wait for the opening credits of Arnie's latest blockbuster? Like I said, I remember the feeling.

Smiley never left me out, no matter how big he got. When Fashion Records employed Alan Edwards as his publicist, Smiley would take me to PR meetings at Alan's plush offices in Wigmore Street. On one such occasion as we approached Alan's office there was a gleaming, slick Mercedes Benz parked outside. We parked behind it and as we walked by to go to Alan's office, we noticed a black man sitting in the driver's seat. I cheerfully commented, 'Respect my brother, your car is wicked, but honestly it's not yours is it?' This totally rubbed the guy up the wrong way, or maybe he was having a bad day. He said to Smiley, "See you Smiley, nuff respect!" but at me he snarled, "You are just a little bwoy". Boy? Little boy! Understand me people this is a big disrespect in the community. I was a grown man who pissed and walked.

I'd paid my dues and earned my rights as an adult, and I was a long time out of kidulthood. Still, I must have touched a button because he was so aggressive in his tone towards me that his bad vibes transferred right back onto me - it's the way these things work. I was still vexed, during and after Smiley finished his meeting. When we stepped outside the guy was still parked up outside the office. As we walked past again to go to my car I gave him the most offensive 'bad man' look I could find in my rude boy locker but my ego was still bruised and I wanted to get even somehow. We drove off and I told Smiley that I was still angry but didn't want to jeopardise his business. He simply said, "Well deal with it then Seny!" With that, I pulled over, got out of the car and collected some bricks from in front of a house that was under construction. I drove back around and parked in my previous parking space behind the Mercedes. I gathered a few of the bricks, got out of my car and made my way to the front of the Mercedes. While walking past the driver's door side I realised the driver was sitting even more comfortably than before, probably reminiscing on how he had just dissed a boy.

As I walked past I grunted, 'Little bwoy? Little bwoy?' I stopped in front of his Mercedes' front windscreen, looked at the driver dead in his eyes and with all the aggression I could conjure, gestured as if to throw the first brick. The manner in which the driver ducked down in his car to protect himself almost gave me satisfaction in itself but I couldn't help myself. I waited for him to look up again. When he came back up I feigned throwing the brick again, and again he ducked down so swiftly that I thought he must have gone through the bottom of the car. I kept him performing his impression of the "now you see me, now you don't" kiddies' game a few more times until I was satisfied that he'd got the message. "Do not underestimate little boys". When I got back into my car, Smiley laughed and said, "I'm sure he knows not to mess with you again". I felt relieved that I'd got that energy out of my system there and then but then started to worry when Smiley received a call from Alan Edwards shortly after the incident. Fortunately my worry was short lived as Alan merely asked about what could possibly have happened. He even made reference to "Asher's lovely, quiet and calm personality." Smiley told him that the guy had upset me and the situation was left at that.

To this day I wonder what big shot that chauffeur worked for, and if he recalls the incident.

It was Alan Edwards who introduced us to the dark arts of public relations, and playing the media game. He even helped get Smiley a part in the British movie Absolute Beginners staring David Bowie and Patsy Kensit. By fair means or foul, he kept Smiley Culture's name current and on trend. When the hits dried up and the Club Mix TV show was out of commission, Alan leaked a story to the media that Smiley had rejected a lucrative role as the villain in Sylvester Stallone's next movie because he didn't want to play the part of a paedophile. That little piece of marketing magic brought Smiley at least twelve months of publicity.

However, the publicity didn't bring a good reaction from certain people who thought that the money generated from the movie could have been used more wisely in the Brixton ghetto. I recall stopping at a shop one evening in Clapham when I was confronted by one of the elder bad boys from Brixton called Fingers. He was fuming after hearing that Smiley had turned down £400,000 and vented at me for a sustained period of time.

I couldn't tell him the story was a hoax so I had to take the intimidation... like a man. When I later told Smiley about this all he could say was, "Well, that's not good. We just better make sure that we're ready for anyone, and at any time then".

The Beat (Dec 84/Jan 85)

New Musical Express (2.02.85)

New Musical Express (4.08.84)

Smash Hits (17/30.01.85)

Smiley sorts out slang

SMILEY CULTURE is the man who rhymed "Leroy" with "Del-Boy."

His record "Cockney Translation" topped the reggae charts for weeks this summer with its mixture of West Indian slang and expressions straight out of "Minder."

By sticking a "my son" in with the "Jah man," it was a musical mini-dictionary that translated Jamaica into Jamaica Road. "Cockney say traffic...We say wassacked!...We say pants, Cockney say strides."

Smiley looks set to do even better with his new release "Police Officer" which has already sold 15,000 and again topped the reggae charts.

It's a tale about being stopped by police who turn out to be fans of "Cockney Translation" and switches scenes from rhyming Rasta to the sound of the "Sweeney."

Smiley said, "I just picked up the idea of

by
CEDRIC PORTER

'Cockney Translation' from the youth. They like changing from one slang into another."

The 22-year-old from Stockwell has worked up his way with words from years of experience deejaying with South London sounds systems.

Regular

His regular partner, Asher Senator (23) said, "It started after school when we used to play records and now and again take the mike and introduce them."

They are former mates

of Tulse Hill and Stockwell Manor schools respectively, and began by working with Buchman Sound, now Studio Mix, in Wandsworth Road.

But it was with Lewisham-based Saxon that they really took off, taking up as a double act the "fast style" pioneered solo by Saxon deejay Peter King.

Smiley claims, "I can probably do about five lines without taking breath.

"Doing the 'fast style' means you have to be really fit. I usually take a run round the block in the

morning and once a week go to the sauna just to relax and have a work-out."

If you can imagine a talking word-processor brought up in Stockwell, you will have some idea of the way the club duo sound.

Smiley's discs and Asher's record "Fast Style Origination" have been brought out on South London's independent Fashion label.

Listening to them, you would never guess that the voicing was done in a converted basement factory at Clapton Junction...

● **DUO DUO**...Smiley Culture (foreground) and Asher Senator get themselves organised for another show.

South London Press: 23rd Nov 1984.

South London Press (23.11.84)

Record Mirror: 26th Jan 1985

The year of the hip hop wallyskankers?

I WONDER how many people are aware that practically the only records in the top thirty not assisted by advertising/promotion are Black Lace's 'Do The Conga', Mel's 'Step Off' and Smiley Culture's 'Police Officer'. These records, have presumably, charted on genuine consumer demand and reflect the nation's un-

hyped taste. What does this say about the rest of the chart? I think we should be told.
Smarmy Bastard, London E2
● Hmm, seems to indicate a strange hip hoppin', skanking, wally shakin' dance alliance the like of which we haven't seen since the days of the late lamented Showaddywaddy

Record Mirror (26.01.85)

New Musical Express (22/29.12.84)

West Indian World (22/12/84)

Below: Smiley and my first ever newspaper interview

Echoes (18.08.84)

Smiley waiting humbly to receive his 3 Reggae awards

Chapter 8

Heads I Win, Tails You Lose

One thing I have to reiterate is that no matter the situation, occasion or circumstance Smiley's competitive edge never left him and he always kept a close eye out for challenges that could generate income. The music industry was just another platform for him to experiment and he never passed up on a good money making or gambling opportunity. Competition became the rule with Smiley and he was happy with any challenge that came his way that involved money. He maintained his commercial instincts and would use me as a secondary option for winning money through friendly gambling.

Ken Hinds was a tall dark, slim but physically fit young man from North London who managed a music publishing company for a Jewish businessman. He was intelligent, educated and very articulate when conducting business. For us it was splendid to see a black man in the position of running a major publishing company that boasted such a healthy budget. So, when he asked us to come to his plush offices in Chelsea so we could sign our publishing agreements, we went without any hidden agenda.

The advance Smiley was to receive for his publishing was in the region of £60,000 whilst mine was a mere £15,000. There was a £45,000 difference in our perceived value but Smiley didn't see it that way and immediately set out to adjust this inequality.

Our lawyers had already approved these agreements so it was all about us signing and receiving our cheques. Ken handed me my agreement and as I was about to sign on the dotted line Smiley briskly interrupted. "Hold on, hold on, hold on. Ken I think you should give Senator more money for his publishing. Senator's big you know and his lyrics are worth much more than what you're paying". Ken agreed with him, but insisted that he couldn't do any better because it was beyond his control. Smiley went further. "Ken, you look strong, can you do press-ups?" Now this had me wondering where he could possibly be going with this because he certainly couldn't do more than ten himself. "I bet you can't beat me at press-ups Ken. How many can you do?" Ken was drawn into the conversation like a fish grabbing the bait that led to its fate and replied, "I'm not gonna tell you how many Smiley, but let's just say I can do a lot".

Smiley said to him "Do you know what? I'm not even gonna challenge you myself, I'm gonna let you take Asher first and if you can beat him, then me and you can do this". That's when I got the drift that Smiley was on another coup. Ken looked at me and as he observed my small frame, I can only imagine that he must have thought it was going to be easy. Ken said he was ready to do this but Smiley went into turbo drive. "Hold on, say you put £2,000 on top of Asher's £15,000 if he beats you, and you can take two grand off if you beat him?" Again, Ken sized me up and definitely fancied his chances as he got up from his desk, took off his suit jacket and started stretching. We heard the clicking of his bones and I thought, 'damn this is like those wrestlers who click their bones to intimidate opponents.' After some deliberation, Ken agreed to go first and set himself in his press-up position. Once more Smiley interrupted "You know what again, press-ups are too easy... I say you guys do one arm press-ups". Ken must have wondered, 'what is this guy on?' but he was already wriggling on the hook and couldn't stop himself. I could see his self-confidence was high and he began his one-arm press-ups to our count of one, two, three, four... He stopped at around fifteen press-ups and Smiley said excitedly, "Step up Seny".

When I got to fifteen one-arm press-ups he allowed me to do two more and then stopped me in my tracks stating happily, "Don't let the opposition see your level". He turned to Ken and stated the obvious. "You better add the two grand to Asher's cheque man!" Ken obliged, albeit somewhat bemused by what had just taken place.

Next on the agenda was the man who owns the Fridge Bar in Brixton, Ralph Daley. At six feet tall and three feet wide, Ralph was not someone to fuck with. He was the head of his own security firm, and they had a good reputation. If Ralph and his team said to leave the club, it was best to leave the club as quickly as you could, without any hint of resistance... maybe even hand them a tip on the way out. Ralph saw himself as the perfect chess player. He visited Smiley's house in Streatham unaware of the situation he was putting himself into. Smiley didn't play chess, but guess what? His sparring partner did and so he initiated a chess match between us. The stake was for £2,000, which I didn't have at the time and so Smiley fronted the amount. In fact, I don't think I would gamble that kind of money even if I had it anyway, losing hurts me too bad. It was best out of three and Ralph had already won the first game.

Funnily enough, he was similar to Smiley in the way that he celebrated after a win and he certainly made me feel uncomfortable with his over-the-top celebrations. I was feeling nervous about Smiley's two grand but he kept on motivating me with comments like, "You've got him right where you want him Seny!" I must say I was totally relieved to win the second game and draw the score to one each. And so the decider began. We were near the end of the game and Ralph had me sweating like a horse. I could see that my next move would be the only move I had before Ralph would certainly claim checkmate. I stared glaringly at the chessboard hoping to see a loophole but the more I looked, the more it seemed impossible to stop Ralph's next move. As I took a final glance around the chessboard my heart skipped a beat when I noticed there was actually a move on for me to win the game. All I had to do was move my castle straight down the column and his king would be trapped, meaning the game would be mine.

But were my eyes deceiving me? My focus was fixated on the board, while in the background I could hear all the voices commenting, none more so than Ralph as he urged me to make my move.

I looked closer at the board and then closer again, and when I was certain that the move was valid I slowed proceedings down even more so I could boast about how to win in style. Then bam, I made the move and yelled in excitement "CHECKMATE!" Everyone was astonished and Smiley and I couldn't hold our laughs as Ralph stood there for a considerable amount of minutes staring at the chessboard, presumably wondering what happened.

Smiley was in full swing now and it seemed as if he was willing gambling opportunities to present themselves. His nephew Merlin loved him and followed in his footsteps as an MC. However, when Merlin completed his recording deal and had just collected a huge chunk of his money advance, he mistakenly came to Smiley's house in Streatham. Smiley had been advising and financially taking care of him from the time Merlin became popular on the UK rap scene but now his protégé was a big star. He came into the house looking like a million dollars and in fact when he actually pulled out his wad of money, it resembled a million dollars.

The wad was of crisp £50 notes and Merlin simply smiled as if it was nothing when Smiley offered him the opportunity to compete with him at blackjack. Merlin was wearing exquisite gold pieces, including a watch, chains and rings. His friend Rudey also wore a gleaming gold bracelet. Smiley couldn't help himself. His commercial instincts kicked in, he baited Merlin and challenged him. "You can never beat me at cards, I never lose, I am the don remember, now face your doom" was the kind of verbal intimidation Smiley used. And so the competition began - £50 a time at blackjack, and Smiley and Asher versus Merlin and Rudey. We sat in our positions in Smiley's sitting room and the card game started. The first few games were evenly matched but then the pendulum swung in Merlin's favour. He started to win game after game and began to mock his uncle laughing aloud and repeating some of the things Smiley had been saying to him earlier. Smiley became frustrated with the constant losses and now needed to sit up straight to try to instil more emphasis into his game. His facial expression said it all as he frowned with anxiety at another loss. Then, out of the blue, Smiley won a game that he wasn't entitled to.

Heads I Win, Tails You Lose

It was the final few cards of the hand and Merlin was beaming in anticipation of another outright win, but to everyone's surprise Smiley yelled, "Last cards and out!" He threw down his two cards and jumped to his feet stating that the tide has now turned. I personally wondered how Smiley pulled that one off and I'm sure Merlin and Rudey did too. Erm... last two cards? Anyhow, the tide did turn and now it was Smiley's turn to win game after game. Merlin became agitated as his money was running out and he tried frantically to regain the momentum. It was to no avail, Smiley won again and Merlin's last £50 was gone, but that didn't stop him. In fact, instead of discouraging him from continuing it seemed to refuel his tank and as he took off his gold chains he demanded in his baritone voice, "Let the game continue". He had the opportunity to change his mind but Merlin and Smiley were made out of similar material and had the same drive. Smiley and I knew this, so unsurprisingly to us Merlin chose to carry on. His three chains were 18 carat gold and each weighed in the region of three to four ounces. As he removed them one by one to hand them over to Smiley he seemed quietly content, as if he was expecting Smiley to give them back in the end.

Smiley though, didn't falter, and continued to win every game with added passion. Merlin went on to lose the three chains, his watch and his rings but still refused to give up the fight. He turned to Rudey and said, "Pass me your bracelet" but Rudey wasn't having it one bit. He looked at his bracelet and said, "What, this? No way Merl" and shied away from the confrontation. Merlin wasn't happy with him one bit and they got into a quick tiff, which led me to think that maybe Merlin bought the bracelet for him in the first place. Rudey held his ground and refused to budge. Smiley took the opportunity to hail his win and shouted, "So that's it then, the game is won".

As he spoke he threw me Merlin's watch and said, "You that Seny!" while Merlin was left pondering on his next move. Merlin turned to him and asked for his jewellery back, but Smiley laughed and said, "You ain't got any bling here, you lost it remember?" Merlin asked me to at least give back the watch but Smiley interrupted and insisted that he would not be happy if I did. He went on to say that Merlin must learn the harsh lessons of life and face up to its consequences. Smiley reasoned that if the shoe had been on the other foot, Merlin wouldn't have returned a thing.

Merlin denied that and continued to ask for his jewellery to be returned but to my amazement, Smiley didn't budge. It turned into a long bout of drawn-out debate that really went nowhere until eventually Merlin and Rudey left. When I said to him, "You're something else!" Smiley replied, "Seny, don't feel any way, Merlin will be wiser for it..."

It was unorthodox, cunning and in some way hard-hitting but that was Smiley in a nutshell. I wouldn't say that he was directly hard-hearted, but when I kept telling him that Merlin was ringing me regularly to ask for his watch, he simply echoed the sentiment that if I gave it back he definitely wouldn't be happy. Yes, it was a tough lesson to learn and at times Smiley could be cold like that, but I had to hand it to him and hailed him as "the original go getter, pace setter, none better".

PART TWO

Reggae Owes Us Money

My phone rang and it was Smiley.

"Seny, I've been done!"

"What do you mean you've been done?"

"I got done, smacked up, gun-butted."

"What do you mean man, who by, when, what's happening?"

"Boy, it was the same guys that came 'round my house last night."

"But they said you had until 6 o'clock today to come up with the money!"

"I know but they came back last night and rushed me."

"That's fucked up, are you okay though, what's up?"

"They bussed my head with a gun handle and punched me up a bit but I'm alright."

"Are you sure you're alright?"

"Yeah man, I'm paining a bit but it's more the situation I'm thinking about."

Reggae Owes Us Money

"What's that?"

"If I don't give them the money by 6 o'clock they're coming back... and I seriously don't have any money Seny."

"Raa, so what, it's a war t'ing yeah?"

"Seny, you saw these guys, they're affiliated man."

"Cha, this is all Gypsy J's fault with them faulty things he gave you. Can't you speak to him and let him deal with it?"

"I know, but you know him, he's snowballing out of this one like an avalanche."

"Dodgy bastard."

"I know... But Seny I'm gonna need your help on this one!"

"What do you want me to do?"

"If you could pawn your chain and pay them out of the money you get, I'll give you back the money soon."

"MY CHAIN? Are you sure Smiley?"

"It won't be for long Seny, you know I got money coming in."

"Yeah, but my chain Smiley..."

"Come on Seny, you know I'll give you back the money to get it out the pawn shop, and I told you it won't be long anyway!"

"Alright, I'll pawn it but please don't take no whole heap a time to get it back Smile."

"I won't Seny, I give you my word!"

"How much do you want me to get on the chain?"

"£2,000."

"Wow."

"Don't worry about it Seny I've got it covered, we'll get back your chain quickly."

"Alright cool, where shall we meet once I've picked up the money?"

"I was hoping that you would take the money straight over to them in North London for me."

"Okay, what's the address?"

"It's..."

Chapter 9

Night Trade

These skills we learn on the microphone are a trade we perfect by night. This lifestyle sucks you in. It starts off innocently, with sweet music flowing from a stereo, and it steals your days. It holds you hostage and just like shotters and pimps, is at its most potent in the small hours. Entertainers mixing with shady characters aren't unique to reggae; it's common to music in general.

One afternoon while chilling downstairs in the studio at Dub Vendor, we both received calls from guys from Brixton who wanted to promote events with us. Messam (bless his soul) was managing Maxi Priest at the time and wanted to book me, while another young man whom I shall call Blitzroy wanted to book Smiley. We invited them over to the studio to make the bookings and when they arrived we conducted the meeting in the live room next door. My business went smooth with Messam, who was an established and respected promoter, and although Smiley's business was also cool I sensed a strange aura coming from Blitzroy.

Still, inside I could feel alarm bells ringing. I sensed trouble because Blitzroy had been acting as if he was superior to Smiley, and a heavy dude worthy of respect. Blitzroy had scheduled his show for a Friday and Beres Bassa, owner of a sound called Moa Ambassa, had asked to include us as special guests on a show at the exact same venue – Brixton Town Hall – due to be held the night before. Smiley informed Beres that he was booked for a show the next night in the same venue so we could only be special guests for sure. This was agreed and everything was cool until a week before the event when Smiley received a phone call from Blitzroy.

He was pissed that Smiley had his name on the flier for the night before, and no matter how Smiley tried to reassure him that it was only as a guest and not as a performer the more Blitzroy was agitated with the situation. He said he was cancelling the show but said Smiley could keep the payment advance until he planned another event and then it could be transferred to the new show. Smiley agreed and was genuinely happy to oblige. However, Smiley called me on the Sunday to say that Blitzroy had changed his mind and now wanted his money back.

He told me that he'd arranged to meet with him the following day at 11 am at Dub Vendor, so he could refund him. That was on the Monday but Smiley had an interview with the Sun newspaper that day, as they were doing a story on the police and their relationship with the black community. That meant he completely forgot about the meeting with Blitzroy. It was a miserable day as well. The rain was pouring down as Smiley took the Sun press team around the community and showed them various hot spots. The interview was dragging on so much that Mikey and I, who were with Smiley throughout the first stages, had to leave him to complete the interview without us so I could get to Dub Vendor for a pre-arranged recording session. Mikey and I left in my Hillman Avenger and when we arrived at Dub Vendor we were in complete shock as Papa Face and John Dub Vendor told us that some guys had jumped over the counter, saying Smiley was hiding downstairs. At that moment the phone rang and it was Smiley's girlfriend. She was hysterical, saying some guys had rushed into her flat and were taking things out. She told us their names and when I heard one particular name I just thought, 'Oh no, this is bad, real bad.'

Night Trade

It was a name I first heard at school – a name that I heard even before seeing the person, and one that was heavily associated with robbing and stabbing. Believe me it wasn't a nice name to have against you. He was a real bad man whose reputation preceded him. I will call him "DW."

We left Dub Vendor immediately and drove down towards the flat in Union Grove. Aware of the category of the people we were about to confront we took off all our gold rings and chains and hid them as we approached the flat. As I drove into the flats, we saw two guys putting items into the boot of a car. We knew instantly that it was Smiley's equipment and so I pulled up quite close to them. When they looked around and saw us they both made their way menacingly towards my car. Blitzroy came around to my side of the car and pacified "Open the window, it's not you, it's just your friend, he left us standing in the rain like pussies so we're just taking things until he comes and pays me my money."

DW, the one with the name that went before him, went to the passenger side of the car and he was also saying that it wasn't us he was interested in, it was just Smiley.

I told Mikey to unlock the door and before I knew it, DW was in the car leaning over to my side with his 007 knife closed, but pointing straight at me and saying in a threatening voice, "Tell your fucking friend to bring the money down to The Hut in Brixton by 7 o'clock tonight because I know where everybody lives and I'll round up a posse and come to everybody's yard!" Displaying a blunt demeanour suggesting that we'd brought this on ourselves, Blitzroy said brusquely, "Make sure" and they left in a hurry.

Lambeth council had given The Hut to the Brixton community after the riots for use as a community centre, although it had since become more of a den for bad men and their street activities. We only passed through The Hut on very few occasions and didn't associate there like we did before, when the front line was further up Railton Road. Times were changing rapidly, hard drugs were flooding the market, and what we'd known as ganja paradise on Brixton Front Line was now a mini drugs city that literally yelled at us to stay away. The Hut was a one-storey building surrounded by a wooden poled fence, with an entrance on Railton Road.

Night Trade

The grounds inside the fence were grass and concrete and it was spacious enough to hold a good quantity of people. Inside The Hut itself, social activities such as pool and card gambling ruled and it was always guaranteed to be full of hustlers.

This was the prehistoric age before pagers or mobile phones so we had to wait until Smiley returned to tell him about what had happened. When he returned and we told him, Smiley went quiet. You could see he was numb, but yet still angry inside. He eventually said, "We can't have this" and with a rebellious spirit, played a reggae track by Jamaica's Half Pint that went, "Ah you lick we first..." I remember thinking 'that's appropriate!' I always knew Smiley did things in a methodical and calculated way, but for him to find a track to coincide with actual events during such a serious situation was audacious. Nevertheless, it motivated the team and we rode out that day in keen anticipation. 7 o'clock had become our "High Noon" and considering that the only real weapon we had was Smiley's old starter pistol, it's a wonder that we were so up for the challenge. As the time drew closer, Smiley picked up the old starter pistol, put it in his waist and said in an emotionless tone, "It's nearly 7 o'clock, let's go..."

By this time Mikey, Fox and I were as ready as could be and even though we possessed an arsenal even the Salvation Army would have laughed at, we still jumped up. Mikey had been involved in an angry dispute with some guys from the same clique prior to that night, and was eager to show them that he wasn't afraid. We arrived across the road from The Hut and seriously, if it was a movie you would hear the suspense music playing in the background. Smiley and I got out and walked over to The Hut while Mikey and Fox waited for us in the car. We knew nearly everyone, so it was natural for us to say hello to a few guys as we entered the grounds. Strangely enough though, everyone we acknowledged either said hello very reluctantly or just ignored us completely as if they all knew what was going on. Blitzroy and DW took us into a long, slim room inside The Hut and asked everyone to leave. When the room finally cleared, Smiley and Blitzroy began to reason.

Blitzroy was saying things like, "Smiley you dissed me and left me in the rain like a pussy, I just want my money..." Smiley replied with things like, "It was an accident. I've got your money so where's my stuff that you took from the yard?"

Blitzroy went on to say, "Your stuff isn't here but I'll get it for you once you give me the money."

While all this dialogue was going on, the room became full of people again and the light was being switched off and on as a scare tactic. I listened carefully as an intimidating yardie leaned over to me and whispered, "Asher, leave this room it's not you, it's Smiley we want". I ignored him, tensed myself within and prepared for the imminent attack I felt was inevitable. It never happened though. Smiley handed over the money and Blitzroy told him that he would have the stuff that they took out of his girlfriend's flat by the next morning. We weren't stupid, that talk was standard "stalling-talk", and we knew they had no intention of giving back the things.

We returned to the car and were further aggrieved to see Mikey being verbally abused by the youths he was in contention with. Although he and Fox were standing their ground we sensed this situation was escalating by the minute. We interrupted the argument and insisted that they all stop this before it goes too far. Then another young man I knew from our Buchanan and Small Axe No. 2 days approached us and while giving me a dancehall flier said...

"Reach to this dance and everything will be okay. This is the Unity Dance, so do this dance and nobody can trouble you again". Whatever! Smiley took the understated but menacing tone in this youth's voice as a direct diss. He said there was no way we could go to that dance as we'd be showing weakness and that would mean these guys would want to be running our careers and lives if we went. Needless to say, but we didn't go.

Around this same time, Smiley bought a blue 7 series BMW that we really believed was jinxed. Someone crashed into it within twenty minutes of him driving it out of the showroom and we certainly knew some local bad boys were deeply envious of it, and haters are going to hate, right? We were in this BMW parked on a side road off Acre Lane, when we saw one of the guys who'd raided Smiley's flat with the youth who'd told me to come to the Unity Dance. Neither of them was happy. They told us they'd lost over £500 because we hadn't turned up to their dance and said we now owed them this money. After pacing up and down the pavement, they suddenly surrounded us. One of them turned to me and said, "Asher you need some chop." That meant he wanted to attack me with a machete but we stood our ground.

Night Trade

There was a lot of eyeballing going on before we backed off into the 7 Series and drove off. We'd already handled a range of challenges and knew our limits but this particular situation was getting real serious, real quick. Plus more and more people seemed to be entering into the equation and so we went to find some people of our own, who could help with our problem. One brother who was a heavy player in the bad man business said to us in a concerned voice, "Who's troubling you?" When we told him the names of the people he just said, "Okay, look after yourselves then" and sheepishly walked off. Rumours were going round that they had guns and we were receiving all sorts of messages about their threats against us but we were determined not to succumb to these bad boys techniques, and looked for ways to defend ourselves. One afternoon Smiley, Mikey, Fox and me were driving into Lansdowne Green Estate and saw a local youth called Sam Dundas. We immediately decided to tell him about our troubles, in the hope that we might receive some salvation somehow. That decision turned out to be one of the most significant choices we'd ever made as it changed the course of events dramatically and led to a whole new chapter in our lives.

We suspected that Sam wasn't a normal nine to five, clocking in and out type of guy but we had no idea of the level to which he was associated with the underworld. He was a short and stocky black guy who spoke with a cockney accent and although we knew him from the area, he wasn't the type of guy that moved in our circles. Sam's lifestyle was different to the average black guy's from our neighbourhood, and none of us knew what he actually did. The good thing was, Sam was eager to help and said he would introduce us to some real, proper gangsters. Of course we didn't hesitate. We accepted the invitation and made our way with him immediately.

We followed him to West Wickham – a leafy town near Bromley, on the outskirts of South London, and then turned into a big drive leading to a beautiful house. The gravel drive had some real length to it and as we drove further it was apparent that the pebbles were getting thicker. The closer we got to the house the more I could hear the pebbles flicking up and bouncing off the tyres and hubcaps. I looked at the house and said, "No way Smiley". It was a Victorian-looking mansion, and big enough to house five sound systems and their members.

Night Trade

Every window had double-glazing and there was intricate woodwork around all the door and window frames. As we pulled up, my attention suddenly switched to the top-of-the-range cars parked in front of the house. I remember taking an extra close look at a BMW on my way past and thinking 'that's some motor!'

Almost immediately, a welcoming party came outside to greet us. A few middle-aged men, a woman and two young teenage boys enthusiastically made their way over to us as we got out of the car. Right away the two boys started saying, 'there's Smiley Culture!' and their fascination rubbed off onto the elders. Someone we deemed as the main man introduced himself as Gypsy J and said to us, "Come inside and make yourselves comfy." When we entered their home, I found the interior lived up to the classy exterior. It was spacious and expensively furnished. Wooden floors, mahogany cabinets and cloth settees met the eyes. The walls were covered with light coloured, rose-patterned wallpaper and had historical pictures of gypsy caravans and traveller sites displayed on them, while exquisite chandeliers hung from the white ceilings. We were invited into the sitting room, which was adjacent to the kitchen.

When I took a quick glance into the kitchen I could see it was also spacious and I immediately caught a whiff of the chicken stew that was brewing. I sat down on one of the settees, soaked it all in and observed. The two teenage boys were around 14 and 16 years old respectively. One of them, the elder looking one, had a bit of body on him while the younger one had quite a lean physique. However it was the younger one who was star-struck to be in the presence of Smiley Culture. He went on and on, saying, "It's Smiley Culture, it's Smiley Culture" until finally he grew tired of that approach and started to follow up strongly with questions like, "How did you make that record?" "Did police really stop you?" "What's a producer?" He was all over Smiley like a rash. Smiley replied as much as he could, albeit somewhat inattentively since he was trying to focus on the conversation that was taking place with the elder gypsies.

All of them looked well fed, with paunchy, potbellied stomachs. Gypsy J's wife was short with a stocky build and we could tell immediately that she wouldn't take crap from anyone. She was assertive in her mannerisms and kept her sentences terse and to the point. She was almost barking orders at everyone, even at us, as she welcomed us into her home.

"Do you want some tea then?" she said to us while making her way into the kitchen. As I looked around the scenery in amazement, I caught a glimpse of Smiley and sensed he was feeling the same energy as me. We were in a place where we only saw interiors like this on TV.

The cool, but direct manner in which the gypsies spoke told us heaps about their realness right away but this didn't faze me, because I was more motivated by the prospect of being able to defend ourselves on a level playing field. It was later brought to our attention that these guys were from the Lewisham gypsy community who'd started out with nothing, hustled in their bare feet and grafted until they made something of themselves. They told us about their relationship with Sam and how close he was to them. They called him their "black son" and didn't hold back one bit in letting us know how tough he was. They showed us pictures of him when he was bare-fist fighting in a gypsy campsite and boasted how he had never lost. The pictures were graphic and grotesque. Blood, cuts and bruises everywhere, and even Sam had his fair share of damage. I looked at him and thought, "Really Sam, why?"

I was becoming aware of how these gypsies loved to talk, and they were really good at it. They were full of blarney and Irish charm, but each gangster tale ate away my fears and lifted my spirits. The more they talked, the more I liked it. When we eventually got an opportunity to tell them about the trouble we were having they started to say things like, "What, from your own? We can't stand people who do their own. Do they stand together? We'll flame-throw the bastards..."

I must admit, it was a comforting feeling knowing that we had an opportunity right in front of us where we could just sit back and let others do the work. These guys were ready. Just a nod from us and they would take things into their own hands. That was a real temptation for us except we knew it was a situation we had to deal with by ourselves, and that our pride and egos dictated that we should stand up and be counted. We let the gypsies know that, and said we just wanted a little encouragement from them. As we continued speaking, Gypsy J sent a man away who returned with two things, one of which had US Army printed on the bottom. We were like "Wow". This was becoming more like a movie with every step. We held the two things and passed them around amongst us.

When Mikey got hold of one of the things he just seemed too comfortable with it until Smiley had to 'dis-thing' immediately. Deep down, all of us were having thoughts of defence and revenge but externally we all kept as cool as we could, so that the gypsies wouldn't class us as, what we really were, gangster novices.

The gypsies were just getting in the swing of things and invited us to follow them to a local pub. We drove our own car and followed them along some dark, winding roads until we arrived at a pub situated in the middle of a small road junction. As we entered the pub with Gypsy J, I took mental note that the pub was full of customers. That wasn't the slightest hindrance for Gypsy J as he took us straight up to the counter and called the pub landlord over to us. Gypsy J said to him, "My mates are in a bit of trouble, do us a favour and give 'em something to get by would ya?" The pub owner disappeared into a back room and returned with a big long thing in one hand and a bag containing some smaller things in the other. I thought, 'Hold on a minute', took another look around to remind myself that the pub was full of customers and then turned my focus back to the landlord who was handing the things over the counter to us.

He was as casually as he'd been serving a pint of lager. This action was accompanied by words of wisdom from the gangster's handbook that went something along the lines of, "If you get stopped by the police, say that I forgot it in your car and as soon as you use it, let me know and I'll report it stolen". This was heavy shit and along with the continued gangster prep talk from the gypsies, we were now ready to take on the enemy eye-to-eye, mano-e-mano. Driving back to town, we were looking forward to putting a stop to the bullyboys throwing their weight around. After we'd arrived, we decided who would have which thing and then we went out looking for the bullies straight away. We didn't see them that night, but now felt a bit stronger for the task ahead. A few days passed and a lot of threats were sent to us via the urban grapevine until one day we saw our two friends who were well known in the community. When our friends saw the unbelievable things we had in our possession they said they were with us and so together we set a plan. Another brethren, Lloydie B wanted to work with us on the matter but we thanked him and told him we were doing this with a small number of people.

He and a few other friends were upset that we were not bringing them in – especially now that we had the resources - but the plan was already set in Smiley's head. He was adamant that we keep it small and that we should simply hit all four culprits who were named so they would know how serious we were. Now we always knew Militant Mikey was, to put it mildly, short-fused and with him being so young there was no way we were going to jeopardise his future. That's why we chose to go on the move without him. This hurt him so badly that when he saw us afterwards he shouted at us so loudly that all we could do was laugh.

We'd set off in a little van with our two trusted friends in the front seats and Smiley and me in the back. We drove around hoping to see one of the bullies and finally saw one of them driving their car in the opposite direction. I rushed out of the back of the van and yelled "Pull over!" He pulled over, got out of his car and with his hand placed inside his jacket as if he had a weapon, made his way back towards us. Smiley said to him "Me hear say you go in mi house." With that, the bad boy looked up to the sky as if he was totally unconcerned and replied, "So whe' you a say?"

Click... Click... Click... but nothing happened, the t'ing stick... stick... stick... All of us looked at each other and I was thinking that before this bad boy can draw his things, something better happen. Anyway, the bully ran in a crouched position alongside the wall and after chasing him for a while we turned around and made our way back to the van. My heart was beating faster than ever before but when we climbed in the back of the van, our two friends in the front seats turned back and shouted "Woy, it's just like Jamaica!" which certainly quelled some of the fear we were feeling. As the van burst through a red light, we were debating whether the bad boy had been hit or not. We thought he must have but then Smiley said, "Let's find the rest of them and finish them so they know how serious we are" and so we drove around the community looking for them. We saw two more of them on separate occasions but the situations weren't right and so we had to let it go for the time being. After we were dropped off at another friend's house out of town, we prepared ourselves for the feedback. When I rang my mum's house in Brixton, my sister told me that some guys came around saying that a notorious man had just been wounded and now it's serious trouble.

Smiley called our friends who'd been driving us and they too, said that three guys came to one of their houses saying that a serious man had been wounded. The difference this time was that our friends told them to "fuck off, and bring who you wanna bring..."

The waiting game was getting too much for us and we needed a draw. We couldn't go back to Brixton so we called a cab and made our way to North London and Omega Studios. Just in case we saw any of our enemies on the journey we decided to take one of the things with us and I didn't feel any way about being the one assigned to carry it. On the way to Omega we fell into another dilemma, since we'd overlooked the possibility of getting stopped by the police. Smiley and I were talking in code about the incident, but the cab driver misinterpreted what we were saying and thought we were planning to rob him, damn fool. When we stopped at traffic lights in North London, he bailed swiftly out of his cab like a paratrooper and called to some police officers who were sat in their car next to us. Smiley immediately jumped out the cab and when the police saw him, they said to the cab driver, "That's Smiley Culture..."

They continued enthusiastically... "He's definitely alright mate, besides if he does anything wrong we'll just go to his house and arrest him". While this was happening all I could do was throw the thing under the driver's seat and hope for the best. However, the cab driver still wasn't convinced and as he opened my door he said to the police, "something's not right" and then started to feel underneath the driver's seat from the back where I was seated. All I could whisper to this cab driver was, 'Please don't hot me up, please!' Either he didn't find the thing or he let me off because he stopped searching and got back in the driving seat. When we drove off, I thanked him anyway and tried to feel for the thing underneath the seat. I must have thrown it so far under his seat that it was out of reach, but as I pushed my hand further I felt it and returned it to my waist. When we got to the studio we were relieved to say the least, but the day's dramas weren't over for us just yet. Omega was a popular spot for Jamaican reggae artists and as we entered the studio it just so happened that there were some yardies flexing their hardcore personalities around us. We tried to ignore their menacing behaviour and continued with the business at hand. We were there to pick up the herb we'd requested and had been left having to wait around.

Night Trade

Every minute that passed seemed an age as the intimidation from the yardies escalated, with some even giving us the scary stare treatment. Smiley had taken the thing from me before going in the studio and decided to act. He strategically dropped the thing on the floor and let them see him pick it up. It was an action to let them know that we were furnished, and weren't easy pickings. Smiley's quick thinking worked a treat as the yardies calmed down and became more respectful towards us. A short time later we collected what we came for and then left. As the days went by the messages came fast and furious. Some were threats and some were just stupid lies, like the one about how they threw cigarette butts at us on Brixton's front line. Never... Anyway, we started to send back some lies too, like the time we saw two of them and they ran so fast, they left their shoes behind. The bad boy who was wounded spread the rumour that we used dummies and that forced us to decide to strike again. One afternoon we stacked up and with Smiley driving, went looking for them on the front line. When we passed The Hut we saw the one who'd been wounded but by the time we parked around the corner and returned on foot he'd disappeared, presumably into The Hut.

We hastily returned to the car, drove around the next corner and were surprised to see the youth who'd demanded that we attend the Unity Dance. We cornered him and he stood there quiet as a lamb as we warned him and his friends to back off, and of the consequences they faced if they continued to fuck with us.

Chapter 10

Que Viva Espana

We were due to perform at two shows in Germany so Smiley took the opportunity to book an earlier trip for five of us to go to Spain. He said we'd stay there for three weeks and then go straight on to do the shows in Germany, meaning we could get a much needed break from all the madness that was going on - well at least that's what we thought. So it was that Smiley, Mikey, Fox, Peter King and me embarked on an episode we'd never forget. We flew to Madrid and Peter King was immediately pulled over by customs at the airport. We waited patiently for the customs officers to give him a thorough search until finally they were satisfied that he was "clean" and we were able to carry on to the city. It was exciting at first but after a few days we found it quite boring and started to ask strangers where the action was in Spain. Benidorm was recommended so we decided this was where we'd go.

Smiley was the one fronting most of the costs and it soon became apparent that it was getting a bit heavy for him to continue feeding five grown men. King and I knew we had some pay to come but that would only be when we got to the gig in Germany, so we started to budget.

On the night before leaving for Benidorm, we'd run out of herbs and decided that we needed to get some. The cabs in Madrid refused to take five of us in one cab and so we took two cabs into the heart of the city. We arrived at this place I can only describe as the equivalent of a high street mall or shopping centre but the difference was it was full of clubs and pubs. All of them were packed and we walked through in amazement, stopping now and again to check out which club we should approach. When we arrived at the last club at the end of the precinct we approached the guys at the door and asked them for some herbs. They said only two of us could go into the club so Smiley and Peter King went in while Mikey, Fox and I waited outside.

After a while, Smiley and King came out hurriedly with some Spanish guys bustling and scuffling behind them. Smiley yelled "We broke off a piece of their hash and they're vex..."

When the guys rushed out behind them, they stopped in shock as they saw three more of us dressed more or less the same as Smiley and King in berets, tracksuits, trainers and gold chains. One of the guys who rushed out was going mad shouting out aloud in Spanish while another was calming him down.

It was quite clear that the guy calming the other was more than likely saying, "Not here but..."

We faced up to them and walked away backwards while trying to keep our composure. By now we were getting pretty good at this form of conflict resolution. We turned the corner and when we were out of their sight, we ran like crazy. We hailed two cabs as quickly as you could imagine, headed back to the hotel and boy did we bu'n that hash contentedly. The next day, we made our way to the airport for tickets to Benidorm but were stunned by the cost to fly or take the train as Smiley's money was running low. We tried a cab and funnily enough, although the cabs in town wouldn't take more than four people, this cab driver said he would take the five of us. We piled our luggage in and on top of the cab and began our journey to Benidorm. We were shocked at how far the journey was but even more taken aback when the cab driver told us how many thousands of pesetas we owed him when we got there. We tried to negotiate with him but he just called over two police officers who simply said to us, "Pesetas pay, no pesetas come with we!" We paid.

Damn, all the good hotels were taken so we chose a small one not too far from the beach. This hotel is not even worthy of a mention much less a description, but ultimately it was a place for us to stay. We put down our luggage and headed for the beach. When we got to there it was like we were known stars although the Spanish people never actually recognised Smiley Culture, Asher Senator or Peter King.

The Spaniards thought we were dancers because of our tracksuits and some went as far as impersonating some crazy dance moves just to impress us. When we told some Spanish guys that we were performing artists, they offered us the opportunity to appear at a local club. We accepted the invitation, but before that we had some sightseeing to do.

All through our time in Spain I kept singing lyrics that included the words, 'Viva Espana' so when we arrived at one of these clubs it was the first thing that I was planning to chat on the mic. However, Smiley and I left the club to pick up something and when we returned, Mikey and Fox told us that Peter had already chatted my idea, and the crowd had loved it... Old thief! Bless up King.

Que Viva Espana

Meanwhile, it so happened that some young local guys kept pestering us on the beach trying to sell us some false gold. Eventually, after they'd approached us numerous times we purchased quite a few pieces from them, just to get them off our backs. Later this false gold, or as they say in Spanish – "ora," was to prove a life saviour to us. While we were out raving one night two Spanish guys came over to us and began to rave alongside us. They told us that they knew all the best spots where the nicest girls partied and said if they could continue raving with us we were guaranteed a proper time in Benidorm. We didn't find any harm in this since we knew their real mission was to hopefully hustle us, and earn some door commission for themselves. It turned out that these two weren't good company and when we linked up with some girls from northern England who took us all back to their hotel rooms for a bit of slap and tickle, nothing of any real sorts happened apart from the fact that the two local guys sneakily stole the girls' purses and disappeared unnoticed. We were totally unaware of them doing such a despicable act but their actions certainly affected us too.

The next night when we arrived at a British based club, the English bouncers on the door warned us, "You guys are in serious trouble. The guys are all down there drinking and they're gonna smash you up."

When the bouncers told us what caused this we immediately realised that we'd been accused of stealing the girls' purses, when it was really those two local thieves. Rather than stay to explain the situation we decided to leave the scene quickly. In fact we thought it best to vacate Benidorm completely. We hurried back to the so-called hotel, seriously sneaked out of there without settling our bill while the receptionist was sleeping and got out of Benidorm fast. After stopping at Alicante, we then took a night train back to Madrid. Those guys could have drank until the cows came home and built up all the aggression they needed, the fact is the only thing they were going to beat up was the memory of us being there.

We stayed one more night in Madrid and went straight to the airport in the morning in the hope of securing transportation to Germany. Money was low, we didn't have enough for plane or train for the five of us and so we decided to try our luck with a cab driver again.

Que Viva Espana

One who introduced himself as Jose agreed to take us, only this time he was going to drive us all the way to Germany. We knew it would be a trek, and probably so did Jose, but none of us could have expected what turned out to be such an incredibly long and exhausting journey. It was ages before we even got to the Spanish border but when we did, the Spanish customs could not believe their eyes at seeing five black guys travelling in one cab. Although they were talking in Spanish it was obvious they were saying for us get out of the car. They took our luggage down, spaced the suitcases out in a line on the tarmac and brought out the drugs' dog, as they do in these situations.

The dog stopped at Peter's case so the customs officer and drug dog went down the line again from the other direction, and again the dog went to his case. For the second time King was searched thoroughly and again nothing was found. Believe me, we interrogated him intensively to find out if he did have anything but he insisted that he didn't. The French customs could see from their side of the border that we'd been taken through the cleaners so I believe that swayed their decision to let us through without any bother.

Que Viva Espana

We journeyed through France for hours but didn't feel as if we were getting anywhere. The countryside looked the same all the way along the motorway and we soon became tired of talking about the same old beautiful view. As the proprietor, Smiley was rightly blessed with the front seat while Fox, Mikey, King and I rotated places around the back seats and floor. The issue was that our legs would become cramped while seated and so we each took turns to sit on the car floor, which was the only place you could stretch out your legs. We kept asking Jose if he was alright because he'd been driving for ages without resting, and I mean night to day to night. Then somewhere in the middle of France on a lonely motorway, Jose decided that he'd had enough. He never really imagined the distance he would have to cover, and couldn't go any further.

For the whole journey thus far, Jose only said, "No problem" so we assumed he couldn't speak or understand English, although we still spoke in Jamaican accents just in case. Smiley was very concerned, as we all were that Jose was going to leave us in the middle of nowhere so he started to work on a plan of action. As we pulled over at a petrol station Jose found another English sounding word in his locker – "directions".

He suspiciously murmured "directions" to us while motioning that he was going to get directions to somewhere. Smiley insisted that the next time Jose stops we should take the car. Mikey was first to agree and King wasn't far behind. He did stop again further down the motorway at another petrol station. King got out of the car, acted as if he was stretching and prepared to drive it away. Jose got out and started talking to the petrol station's attendant. King jumped in the left-hand drive vehicle, slammed the driver's door shut and headed towards the motorway.

When we hit the motorway, I thought let me look back to see where Jose was and, to my complete astonishment, little Jose was hanging at the back of the car shouting, "Policia! Policia!" His hair was blowing back ferociously and his eyes were barely open as the wind was overpowering him. We told King to pull over and he did. Jose ran to the driver's side of the car but as that was the side where I was sitting, I quickly locked both doors. King kicked down again, and again Jose held on for dear life, his grip helped by the ropes we'd used to tie our luggage onto the car. King said, "I'll throw him off" and everyone yelled "NO" as King began swerving the car left to right.

We forced him to pull over and Jose ran to the driver's side again. He was saying, "No problem". I had an idea and started to hit King whilst shouting at him, "Are you crazy, are you sick..." I turned to Jose and using extreme body language said, "He is mad, we are sorry. He is a mad man, you understand..." The others joined in and started shouting at King. Jose was calm as he coolly got back into his driver seat saying, "No problem". The time was around 5 am and it was becoming light on the motorway when we saw a police van. Jose flashed them to pull over, said to us, "directions" and went over to the police van, this time taking his keys with him.

He came back and said, "No problem" and began to drive again. We were puzzled and enquired amongst ourselves whether Jose bought it or if he was playing us. Either way, the ball was in his court. After a while he turned off the motorway and drove around some back streets until he came to a police station. He still said, "directions" and went into the police station while we were left in the car contemplating the situation, which we identified as being real bad. We couldn't run and leave our luggage, and even if we did, where were we anyway?

One policeman peeped out of the police station and after taking one look at us, called for what seemed like every police person on duty in the station. In minutes we were in the reception area of the police station. Smiley tried to talk to the large looking police chief at the desk but he shouted something in French that meant, "Sit down over there". I remember thinking, 'shall I cry now?' as I looked around at the dirty state of the reception area, and my mind started to imagine what the cells would look like. Jose was at the reception desk complaining away, but there 'WAS PROBLEM'. The desk sergeant could not understand Spanish and Jose could not speak French, so there was no verbal communication going on. A few months previously, Smiley had performed 'Police Officer' in France, on a TV show that was the French equivalent of Top Of The Pops. Smiley took out the single and caught the attention of the French police chief, who called him over to the reception desk. We all quickly followed. It was amazing as the police chief looked at the record sleeve and laughed, as if insinuating that he knew it. Now we were still having difficulties communicating and so we made sure that we approached every police officer who came into the station, and asked them if they could speak English.

Jose followed our lead and asked every officer if they could speak Spanish. After some time, a young female officer arrived and when we asked her if she spoke English she replied that she did, but only a little. We were overjoyed and, while Jose was still irate and trying to get his point across we immediately explained our side of the story to her, which she translated to the police chief.

We stuck to our story that Jose wanted to dump us in France because he was tired and we continued explaining that it was a big problem for us as we could only pay when we got to Germany. After hearing our version of the story and while still not being able to understand what Jose was so irate about, the police chief decided that we should pay Jose up to this point so he could return to Spain. This left us with another problem as the little money that Smiley had was not even enough to get us all food, much less get us to Germany. Still, we decided to barter with Jose and Smiley offered him the little money he had. This irritated Jose even further and so we offered to pay him the remainder in gold. No don't be silly... Not our real gold but the gold that we bought from the young hustlers on the beach in Benidorm – the totally false "ora".

Jose examined the gold very closely and did seem suspicious of it at one stage but I believe his greed clouded his uncertainty and he accepted the deal. He still wasn't finished with his complaints however, and continued to show the police his knees, while insinuating that the drag marks on his trousers were caused by us trying to take his car.

His attempts were passionate but they were in vain because the police just couldn't understand what he was saying and when they asked us what he could possibly mean, we just said we didn't know what he was talking about. Eventually Jose seemed to be satisfied with the outcome and what he thought was a good deal. Finally, the police ended up escorting us to the train station and even advised us to beware of robbers. What a palaver! But it was a beautiful day to walk away from what could easily have been a total disaster. Even now I still can't believe that we could imagine for even one second that we could get away with taking Jose's cab.

Can you picture it now... five black guys in a car with a Spanish registration driving in the middle of France at odd hours of the morning with luggage on top of the roof and more strapped to the back?

Que Viva Espana

Boy, the only destination we would have been going was straight to jail so thank you, thank you, thank you our guardian angels. I still shudder to think what Jose thought and felt after he got back to Spain and checked his haul, only to find the gold was false. Hopefully though, deep down, he understood that we were working strictly off survival instincts.

Our next move was to try and raise some funds so we could continue our quest to reach Germany for those shows. Previously in France, Smiley and I had met some good music people who owned a record shop in Paris and so we decided to head there in the hope that these people could help us. A lady by the name of Fanny was one of the directors at the record shop, which was called Blue Moon. We were happy to say the least that she was at the record shop when we arrived. We told her our plight and she loaned Smiley the money we needed to get to Germany. I can't quite recall if Smiley eventually paid them back the money but something in my memory bank tells me that he did. I hope so anyway because the money they lent us served a big purpose and we used it wisely. Some of it was used to pay for our stay in a decent hotel while the rest covered the fare for a sleeper train to Germany.

When we arrived in Germany we were greeted by the promoters and taken to our hotel. It was a relief for us to actually feel relaxed for a while. We'd arrived the day before the shows were scheduled and so we used the down time to just chill and give thanks that we made it. The next night when we arrived at the club for the first show it was an instant reminder to us of why we loved the music business so much. The club was called Gentle Club, and attracted young German women and UK soldiers based in Germany. Whilst quite small it was guaranteed to be packed for our two shows, and we were more than ready. It was great to get back to what we did best and when we got onto that stage, the appreciation we received from the audience of squaddies and frauleins was on another level. King and I were the main performers on the first night and Smiley controlled the second night while Mikey and Fox shared the mixing duties. There was so much positive energy around that we chatted a bombardment of lyrics for the fans – lyrics like my 'Nuclear Weapon Radiation', King's 'Step on the Gas' and Smiley's 'Police Officer'. We enjoyed these shows in such a way that we became fans of our fans and we meant it sincerely when we promised them that we would be back soon.

After it was over we received our pay from the promoters and then faced reality as we prepared for the task ahead, of going back home to the turmoil that we'd left behind. Throughout the whole trip, whenever we had the chance we always phoned home to find out what was happening, but we never got any news that worried us too much so we enjoyed our time in Germany, and put the south London soap drama to the back of our minds. Unfortunately, we were about to find out just how hostilities really stood.

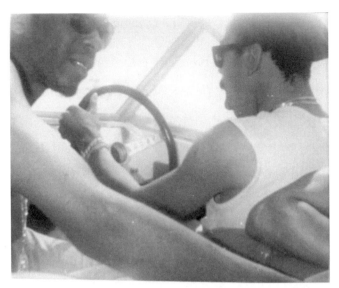

Smiley driving speedboat in Benidorm while Peter King looks on

Smiley and Asher in French police station with French cops

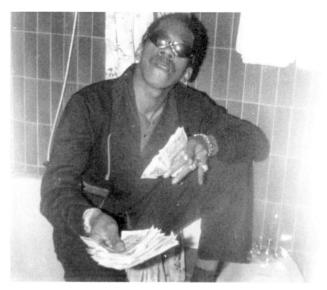

Hotel in Paris: Smiley counting the money that we loaned

Hotel in Paris: Smiley and Asher mean business

Hotel in Paris: Smiley and Asher finding something funny

Peter King, Militant Mikey, Asher Senator and Fox in Gentle Club
in Germany (picture taken by Smiley)

Chapter 11
Turbulence

When we returned to Brixton, the talk on the road was that the enemy were planning to hit Smiley at the first ever UK Reggae Sunsplash, due to be held at Crystal Palace's football ground. Everywhere we went people were warning us not to go to the event as they emphasised how serious the threat level was. Smiley spoke to David Rodigan, one of the main organisers of Sunsplash and explained the situation to him. As we listened at the other end of the phone, Rodigan expressed concern and gave reference to how tight security would be but we couldn't afford to take any chances. We called our gypsy friends and they didn't hesitate in agreeing to act as our personal security at the Splash.

When the day finally arrived we met up with the gypsies near Selhurst Park stadium, as the plan was for all of us to make our way in together. To our surprise the gypsies were only five-man handed, which didn't bode well with our already twitchy nerves. We knew that the enemy would have scores of people with them and so we asked the gypsies where the rest of their guys were. They confidently assured us that they had the equipment and they knew how to handle any number of men.

This helped us to trust in these five gypsies and we subsequently felt more comfortable having them alongside the five of us. When we got to the backstage area I remember Rodigan taking a look at the gypsies and saying to us "Heavy guys".

Smiley was as nervous as me and kept asking if I'd seen any of the bullies. I hadn't but he reminded me to stay vigilant, saying that he really didn't want to perform but knew he was at the point of no return. The host called his name and the crowd was ecstatic baying for their own homegrown, Cockney Translator to grace the stage. Looking at me he said, "Here goes Seny... stay as close as you can..."

He took to the stage and I could see the tension gripping his entire body. I shouted "Gwan Smiley, you a the don. Mash this up!" My intention being to encourage him and squash the negative energy he was feeling. I don't know if it helped but that's how we showed our support for each other no matter the weather. We were both dressed in army greens and while he was performing I made sure that I stood right there on stage. My hand placed firmly in my waist, face wrangled with attitude and my eyes fixed on the crowd like a hawk.

Turbulence

A security person must have wondered who I was and came over to tell me to leave the stage, but my belligerent reaction ensured that he left me alone. By any measure, it wasn't one of Smiley's better performances but that was understandable given the circumstances, and he was the first to admit that he could have performed better.

Having completed the show safely, our goal was to leave the event in the same manner – i.e., safely. While we were backstage saying our goodbyes I noticed a producer from Jamaica called Fatis making his way towards us in his usual 'threatening' style. Fatis, bless his soul, was a big man with a stature of at least six feet or more, while our gypsy friends all averaged about five-foot seven or thereabout so you can imagine that it was quite a sight when Gypsy J mistook his approach as hostile and made his way towards Fatis saying, "Is this one of 'em, is this one of 'em?" We said no and Gypsy J relaxed.

As a matter of fact we didn't see any of the enemy until we were outside. When we walked away from the stadium we looked back and saw that we were being followed by some of the people rumoured to be looking for us.

There were about twenty or so of them but our gypsy friends simply ordered us to, "Turn, face 'em and stand firm!" The ten of us stood there looking straight at them and after a standoff that lasted a few minutes they eventually turned away and moved out. What an experience! It was quite daunting but it certainly showed them that we'd defend this thing until the end.

Gypsy J went on to hail that day as historic and continually used it to blag to his gypsy compatriots as the day they helped Smiley Culture against fifty thousand blacks at Reggae Sunsplash. We just took his embellishment with a pinch of salt because we thought he was entitled to boost his ego after the real help he gave us.

Gypsy J and the gypsies never asked us for any money for their support, but we should have known there's no such thing as a free lunch. The dangers of the battle with the enemy lingered on, although our national and international workload saw to it that we were hardly around the area. Still, we had to be diligent and fully aware, as we knew that if any of us were caught slipping it could be curtains for us.

Turbulence

At this stage we were carrying protection with us everywhere until one day Smiley was driving on his own in Stockwell. Two police officers seemed to be purposely waiting for him on one of his usual routes and jumped out to pull him over.

Smiley told me afterwards that the way the police officers leapt out into the road in front of his car, he was forced to break suddenly and his thing, that was under the driver's seat, flew forward and hit his feet on the pedals. He said he had no time to re-hide it as the police officers were already at the car windows.

Maybe in another situation I wouldn't write exactly what Smiley was arrested for but because the incident was reported on television news and printed in the Sun newspaper I might as well. The police charged Smiley with possession of a firearm and this was as serious a crime back then as it is now. The only difference being that you'll receive a bigger sentence nowadays, yet when Smiley went to court he only received a £450 fine. A £450 fine you might wonder... Well yes, but what did you expect? Because Smiley told a story that nearly had the court in tears.

He told them that some boys from around the area were trying to extort money from him. True, and this was already on their records as his girlfriend had reported the incident when they stormed into her flat. Smiley went on and said that he was in a pub drowning his sorrows one night when some guys approached him, saying that they had heard about his troubles. False. He said they offered him a replica gun and he took it because he wanted to frighten the bad guys off. False. He swore that he never knew the gun was real. False. The beauty of it was that Smiley ensured his story sounded real and with that, he was fortunately given the benefit of the doubt by the courts.

After Smiley's run in with the law, we accepted that it was way too hot for us to be carrying our things and so we had to move more wisely, and someone else carried them instead. Happily for us, after a few more encounters and stand-offs with the enemy, things began to calm down a little. I believe that the resistance we were putting up finally discouraged them as they realised we were not the easy-pickings they thought or hoped we would be. Regardless of the outcome, this entire madness seemed to invigorate Smiley as he embraced more of a gangster mindset.

He boasted to friends, visitors and anyone he thought to be worthwhile about how we chased off bullies and were real gangsters. Of course I joined in most of the time as Smiley always sought my confirmation by saying, "En' it Seny..."

He also embraced the friendship of the gypsies and we continued to visit them and they us, building up a stronger bond of trust. In fact, the scenarios that we went through with the gypsies is a whole other story – the cons, the acts, the disagreements and the earnings all contributed to what was quite an exciting, but iffy period in our lives. We didn't class all the time we spent with the gypsies as turbulent. In fact some remarkable and great things materialised from that period as well. One time Gypsy J introduced us to someone who was even higher in the clique than himself, who I shall refer to as Carly Givemsum. Carly and Gypsy J invited Smiley to a meeting in New Cross at their car showroom. I waited in the car while Smiley was inside for at least two hours. Finally he came out and told me that we were going to build our music studio in the basement of their car showroom. So said, so done. We built our studio there and Smiley decorated it immaculately with top quality equipment and furniture.

Turbulence

He'd met a highly skilled studio technician and engineer by the name of Tim Owen, who'd done an excellent installation of the original studio and so Smiley always ensured that Tim remained as his technician. The studio in New Cross was our step-up to the next level in the music industry. Smiley enjoyed kitting it out with light-brown, wooden wall panels, a luxurious carpet and top-of-the-range equipment. A long corridor led to the room where the console was stationed, and there was a generously sized voicing and live room area.

The kitchen area was as equally lavish as anywhere else in the studio and even the toilet reflected the lengths that Smiley had gone to in maintaining the high standards he demanded. The toilet had the same wooden panelling as the rest of the studio and was so cosy that we'd have to knock on the door and ask if people were okay, because they'd sometimes spend so long in there. Peter King was a man of many skills so Smiley employed him to mount the wall panels but then when he took too long to pay him; King went ballistic and punched through one of the panels he'd built. I was glad when this was eventually resolved, with King having agreed to fix the panel and Smiley ensuring that he'd pay him on time in future.

Turbulence

As our relationship with the gypsies grew stronger, our trust in them and their judgment grew too. One morning when we arrived at the studio they came downstairs and informed us that the police had raided the car showroom earlier that morning. They said they'd discovered some police bugs with their surveillance detector gadget and needed to check out our area too. No bugs were found in the studio but the fact that they were operating at that level served to remind us of the league we were involved with. Smiley told me that the gypsies had made him a proposition to earn some real money by investing some of his own. The deal was that Smiley would invest £25,000, and then in two weeks' time he would receive his money back, along with £100,000 on top. It was irresistible and even though they didn't say what the deal entailed Smiley was more than tempted to engage. People – if something sounds too good to be true, then it usually is. He asked me whether or not he should do it but I mostly answered with statements like, "It sounds serious" and "imagine that!" Smiley was the master of shaping rhetorical questions but on this occasion it seemed as if his mind was already made up, and he was going to invest his 25 smacks.

Turbulence

After we left the bank on the day he was to invest his money and were on our way to the car showroom, Smiley asked me once more if I thought he should do it. The reason why I never directly said yes or no was because I didn't want to be blamed if it went wrong and believe me, he would have done just that. Again I waited in the car for him while he went in to do the business and when he came out he told me what happened. Before he started explaining he showed me a small package and said they had given him some cocaine so I immediately said, "Dash that!" I reminded him that we are Ribena and sensimilla people and so as we drove along the New Cross Road, Smiley held the small packet out of the car window and we watched the ingredients blow away like snowflakes swirling in the wind. He then told me that he'd invested the £25,000 and how in two weeks we were going to have some serious money to play with. He said everything was good, because Gypsy J had guaranteed that he had it covered if anything went wrong. Two weeks later and word came back that there was a delay. Now this delay that the gypsies spoke about stretched week after week until around the sixth week, Smiley had had enough and went to confront them.

Turbulence

Gypsy J had already been kind enough to invite us to his new house in East Grinstead, Surrey and we were genuinely mesmerised by its beauty as it stood alone in the middle of woodlands, and looked like it cost a mountain of money.

The turning into the long drive from the A22 was so small you needed to slow down from way before or else you'd miss it. It certainly hid the fact that further down the drive there was a luxurious home within the grounds. The house was twice the size of the one in West Wickham and to top it all, it had an indoor swimming pool, a dog-racing track, stables and ponds. It was easily worth millions and what made it even more appealing in our eyes was the fact that Gypsy J welcomed us with open arms, letting us know we could visit or even stay anytime we wanted. Yes, we were happy for Gypsy J and his family, but there was something yelling out to Smiley and I at the back of our minds about the timing of his purchase. Could he? Would he? Did he? Nah, he could never, or maybe he could have. Well that's exactly what was going through Smiley's mind as he weighed up the odds of the possibility that the gypsies may have scammed him. Smiley remained hopeful that he'd get his money soon and upped his game.

Turbulence

We kept going to Gypsy J's house but all we received was story after story of why and how the deal went wrong. He told us that the man who was the main operative in the deal had been busted by customs and so they had to keep everything quiet for a while. He used the frightening technique, saying that he hoped the man would not grass because everyone would be in the shit. "And you don't want that, do you Smiley?" He even went on to say that the man had three young children and a wife to support and a mortgage that needed paying while he was gone and "What, are you gonna help to support 'em with us Smiley?" All he was saying pointed to the fact that they'd probably conned us and Smiley wouldn't be receiving his 25 grand anytime soon. One day Smiley called me complaining about the money and saying that he had a plan to get it back.

He said we should pay Gypsy J a surprise visit and with that, we decided to take Smiley's apprentice Paul Culture ("PC") along with us. Now PC had a kind of mean look about him so we thought this may put the shakes up Gypsy J a bit and trigger him to release some money back to Smiley. Now PC may have appeared mean with his hard-looking exterior but on a real level he never had any bad boy credentials or reputation.

It meant the first thing we needed to do was make him feel comfortable about the situation. We told PC that some silly guy had some money for us who thinks he's a gangster but is really an idiot, and with that we encouraged PC to just look as if he was hard. When we pulled into Gypsy J's drive and the three of us got out of the car, he came over to us quite quickly and moved towards PC first who was standing there looking hard, but Gypsy J challenged the intimidation. "Who's this then? What, you want some do ya?" We quickly intervened and aggressively as he could, Smiley said that he wanted his money. Gypsy J replied, "I told you I ain't got any money so what do you want me to do, shit it?"

What a phrase! It pissed us right off at the time but we actually went on to use it a few times. "What do you want me to do, shit it?" Anyway, we never got any joy on that trip and to make it worse, PC was properly vexed on the journey home saying, "That was a real gangster wasn't it?" and "You lot are fucked up" as we sat there laughing like crazy. Smiley gradually began to accept the fact that he would never get his £25,000 back, and so he adopted a "if you can't beat them, join them" mentality and decided to work with them.

Turbulence

The gypsies always had deals going on so the objective now for him was to ensure that he got his money back by using a different method. He certainly made back some of his money from them but the continuous, underlying thing with the gypsies was that you had to be very careful because they'd take you again while you thought they were working with you. Their motto was once they took from someone they never gave back and their reasoning was that they didn't like greedy bastards – go figure.

Smiley was threatened by unhappy business associates on several occasions and more than once he was physically attacked after people thought that he'd conned them. I've already mentioned the time when he rang me up one morning, saying he'd been done and needed to raise £2,000 in a hurry. Apparently he'd attained some dubious particulars from Gypsy J and transferred them onto this notorious "shotter", or gunman. When it all came out they demanded their money back and Smiley received a beating from them in the process. When I saw him afterwards I was relieved to see that he hadn't been hurt that badly, and the physical damage wasn't too noticeable.

His forehead contained a coco where he said the guys had gun-butted him but other than that his pain was mostly emotional. Later in the day I pawned my chain and made the journey over to north London to pay the money for him. When I got there I went into a small warehouse and made my way upstairs where I was greeted by a small woman who appeared to be a receptionist or secretary of some sort. She exuded professionalism as she welcomed me happily while calling the guy on the phone. He answered and spoke to me in a manner that sounded regretful. I remember him saying consolingly, "Asher, I didn't want to hurt him but he took too long with the money. I told him that the people I work for aren't nice guys but he didn't listen". I expressed my concern with regard to the actions he'd taken and he even went as far as saying sorry. I then handed the money to the lady, who thanked me and I left. While driving back to south London I kept thinking about the sincerity in the guy's voice when he'd apologised. It had me wondering, 'Why would someone go so far, only to be so regretful?' He could have been scared of retaliation from Smiley, or maybe he was so high on drugs at the time that he hadn't known what he was doing.

Or it could simply have been the truth when he said that the guys he worked for didn't mess around and posed a serious threat to his life. Whichever one it was, I was glad for this whole episode to be resolved. Smiley was too, but he was still intent on following through his purpose to get some payback from Gypsy J.

While Smiley focused on implementing his "payback" mission I kept my eyes firmly on the prize and continued to remind him about my chain. After a few weeks had passed I had to change the tone in my voice to a harsher sound to bring Smiley's full attention to the fact that I really wanted my chain. Somehow he found the money right away and while passing it to me said, "Get your chain rude boy!" Smiley wanted to hold on to the money longer to conduct more business but with every day that passed, the fears that I may not see my chain again increased. Still, he wasn't deterred by the unpleasant experience and began to implement his own cons on people. He followed the gypsy style of hitting the toughest guys because they would struggle to come to terms with the fact that you had the minerals to attack the boss.

Smiley was also working off the gypsy logic that if someone doesn't hit back straight away it becomes all talk after that and they'd never hit back at all as their anger diminished with time. Smiley mirrored their actions so much, he became a mini version of them in the way he conducted his business operations, and he definitely made sure that he used some of their philosophies to his benefit.

He pulled off some little scams for himself, as if to test the waters, and made money but it also brought more trouble for him. In fact the trouble even circled me too at times when people who could not find him approached me and expressed their anger to me.

Down to things such as £50 notes, people would ring me up complaining how Smiley had laid a dodgy one on them, Smiley found it funny. My phone rang late one night and it was the dread Benji from Brixton. He was fuming as Smiley had laid a dodgy fifty on him. I gave him Smiley's number and thankfully they sorted it out. Vincent, from Brixton approached me menacingly and with a vengeful tone insisted that if he didn't get his money from Smiley it would be serious repercussions for everyone. Smiley was even kind enough one day to call me and dupe me into being involved in a coup that I had to go along with because if I dithered and stuttered whatsoever, there would have been blood spilt on the spot.

Turbulence

Smiley was a don when it came to holding his nerve and so it proved time after time when guys with hard or even gangster reputations quizzed him on what exactly happened to their money. Smiley also used Gypsy J and the Gypsies in some of his coups because he knew that extra muscle acted as a deterrent if rude boys wanted to kick off about their money. Looking back now and actually writing about it has made me class those specific times as real turbulent, even though back then I totally embraced the vibes of the Gypsies. Artistically, this was a big turning point in our careers but unfortunately, we forgot about the thing that made Smiley that money in the first place... lyrics. Contrary to previous years, rather than using this experience as motivation to write some serious rhymes, it caused another psychological dent in our creativity. The wheel of life was definitely drifting in the wrong direction.

Chapter 12

Kingston Hot

We had the universe at our feet - it was there for the taking. Lyrics were king, we were exporting our brand of rhyme-making wholesale and the people loved it. No more so than in the home of reggae music, Jamaica. To think that we started out trying to emulate our heroes on the microphone and now Jamaica was mad for our style. The tables had turned but we were so deep into our own thing, we didn't or couldn't appreciate what was really happening to the music on a global scale.

Rock music was on its last legs, there was a backlash against funk, and jazz with its niche and elitist following had seen its golden age. Pop and R&B was in dire need of a re-boot as they were beginning to sound too structured and formulaic, and there was a highly publicised disco demolition. People burnt disco records on mass in the centre of a baseball field. The tectonic plates of music were shifting and the youth of the day were waiting for the next big thing.

Meanwhile we kept things moving and more often than not, Smiley acted spontaneously.

When he heard Maxi Priest, Tippa Irie and some other UK artists were to perform at Reggae Sunsplash in Jamaica he said, "We're going" and so said, so done. Smiley paid for my ticket, I covered my expenses and zoom we were on our way to the birthplace of reggae music for the first time. That trip was an adventure. It proved to be an unforgettable experience for us and the excitement began on the plane itself. The world was a different place back in 1985 and smoking was allowed everywhere – in offices, shops, restaurants and even airplane flights, can you imagine? On this particular flight ganja was bu'ning on the plane before we even reached halfway to JA. At one stage we looked at each other and asked, "Can you smell ganja?" We made our way to the back of the plane to find a whole load of people smoking and drinking, having a wonderful time as if they were in a dance. We were shocked to say the least but obviously we joined the party. Our plane landed in Montego Bay and we prepared to step out onto Jamaica soil. The stewards opened the door of the plane and I remember feeling the heat instantly. As the perspiration started to drip down the sides of my forehead I looked at Smiley and saw that he was as drenched as me.

He had droplets of perspiration along the front of his forehead and as he wiped it with his flannel (it was a style back then, for men to walk with face flannels poking out of their back pockets), more beads of sweat appeared right away. "It's hot Seny," he said and we laughed.

The passage through to customs was chaotic as we shuttled with the crowd and the constant wave of heat engulfed us. By now, I was perspiring all over my body and couldn't wait to get out of the airport. Finally we emerged at the other end of customs and took in our first glimpse of Jamaica. Immediately, we were rushed by hustler porters who wanted to carry our luggage and me being me, I gave one of them my suitcases and said, 'Follow me.' Smiley didn't agree with me doing that and asked why I did it. He knew that the hustler would be asking for a ridiculous tip and he wasn't about to let anyone take us for granted. When the hustler asked for the money, Smiley gave him what he thought was sufficient and told him to be cool. The hustler asked me if I could do a little better and with that he ended up with two tips for one job.

Anyhow, we were in Jamaica and ready to 'Jam'...

Kingston Hot

Now we knew Maxi Priest and the other UK artists would be staying in the Pegasus Hotel in Kingston and so our mission was to head straight there. We jumped in a cab and began our journey through the beautiful and scenic countryside of sweet, sweet Jamaica. As soon as the cab driver turned out the airport we asked him to find some ganja for us and he stopped at a shack at the side of the road. Now the ganja was nothing special and didn't deserve writing home about but it was about to serve its purpose. We built up our spliffs and even though the taste was weak and left us wanting for a buzz we still smoked them joyously, while expecting something magical to happen. Then kaboom! I don't know whether it was the side effects or after effects that had me feeling sick, but all I knew was that it wasn't good. My stomach churned with pain and I felt weaker by the second. At one point I felt so bad that I actually thought that I might die in Jamaica and I hadn't even seen any of the island yet. The cab driver took the initiative and pulled over again, this time at a fruit shack. Smiley bought a bunch of bananas and as I ate the first one I started to feel better. I ate about six bananas and recovered like a hero, which still has me respecting the nourishing, healing powers of bananas to this very day.

Although that still doesn't mean you can throw them at me if I'm playing football – I wouldn't be happy about that at all. As our cab pulled into Kingston, I saw the difference in the environment. There were still people living in shacks but as we moved further into New Kingston it was like another country, and the investment in development was prominent. We booked into what was then called the Wyndham Hotel, which was just a stone's throw away from the Pegasus. We were now ready for whatever Jamaica had in store for us, so "bring it on" was the cry. One of the first things we did was ask the Jamaican hustlers who stood outside of the hotel to find the reggae singing legend Barrington Levy, as we previously sparred with him many times in England. Like Smiley, Barrington had recently had a crossover hit in the British pop charts called 'Here I Come'. At least three of the hustlers made off straight away – each of them claiming that they could locate Barrington easily. While we were in our hotel room, one of them returned, informing us that Barrington would be with us soon. We peeled off a change and gave the hustlers some US dollars to share between them; then made ourselves comfortable in our 5th floor suite that consisted of two double beds, a luxury shower and a small balcony overlooking the main road.

We were more than happy chilling and running joke upon joke when the phone in our suite rang. When I picked up the phone I was amazed to hear the receptionist say in her sweet, smooth Jamaican accent, "Mr. Senator or Mr. Culture, you have a guest downstairs". It was the man himself - Mr. Barrington Levy just as the hustlers had promised. When Barrington entered our suite he immediately asked us where our big gold chains were and was amazed when we told him that we'd put them in the hotel safe in reception, like the other tourists. Upon settling a little from frantically laughing about it, Barrington told us straight. "Yow, you're stars so put on your chain dem. No bwoy can't trouble your t'ings" and with that we immediately collected our bling on our way to hit the road with Barrington.

Barrington was with his younger brother who he'd kitted out with gold chains and rings. He pointed towards his four-door rental car and we jumped in – Smiley in the passenger seat and Barrington's brother and me in the back seats. Barrington drove and at first Smiley and I thought he was trying to impress us with his erratic driving antics but as time progressed we realised that Barrington was just being Barrington.

Like so many of the drivers in Jamaica, the road safety code didn't apply to him. Most of the time he drove at speeds you'd only associate with a James Bond car chase, and other times he reversed so fast that even cars going forward would have found it difficult to keep up with us. On top of that Barrington had a playful and mischievous nature, and always meddled in other people's affairs. The time that shook us up most came when we had to pass a police blockage in the road after we'd left Kingston and were heading for Mo'bay, where Reggae Sunsplash was taking place. Two uniformed police officers were occupied with people they'd already stopped but Barrington slowed down and cheekily asked, "Whe dem do officer?" Now when these police officers turned and zeroed in on us, taking in the amount of gold we were wearing they just said, "You pull over too!" I couldn't help but think, 'Why did you do that Barrington?' All I knew was that Smiley and I were about to experience for ourselves one of those moments we'd often heard about, and what Jamaican police can put you through. I was admittedly shook up and boomy... Cha, scared. As we pulled over on the left and were waiting for the officers to complete their check on the other car, we saw another person walking towards our car.

Now I say person because the way this man looked, it had us questioning each other as to who he could possibly be because he had dirty – and I do mean dirty – clothes; very picky – and I do mean *very* picky hair – and flaky dry skin. He truly looked like he hadn't just spent the one night, but maybe his whole life living in the bush. He was also armed with a machine gun, which we later found out was an M16, and as he came closer to us I remember looking back for the uniformed officers in the hope that they would come and save us from this murderer. He walked up to the car and yanked open Smiley's door while bluntly stating, "Oonoo come out a de car". Before we could even make a move he repeated himself, saying harshly, "You no hear whe' me say? Oonoo come out a de car!" When we realised that he was a plainclothes police officer we couldn't get out of the car quick enough. His mood was rotten as he started searching the car, beginning with the passenger seat where Smiley was sitting. As he leaned into the car we got a glimpse of the handgun that was shoved in the back of his trousers, in his waistband. Ironically, Smiley had collected some money from the bank that he'd had transferred from England and it was in a money pouch right where the policeman was searching.

He opened the bag, saw the US dollars, looked back at us as if to say, "I'd love to take this" but with that he closed the bag and returned it to where he found it. He looked at us again, then went over to a fence and leaned there with one foot kicked up on the fencepost while just staring at us. The uniformed officers came over, participated in some banter with Barrington and eventually cleared us to drive on. When the car began to drive I looked at the plainclothes officer and made a peace gesture but he just stared right back at me without any expression or movement. I said to the others that I hated to imagine what he would be like if he stopped us with his friends on a dark night.

When we got to Reggae Sunsplash the first thing Barrington did was approach a policeman and take the liberty of adjusting this officer's gun on his hip. Barrington quipped, "Fix your gun officer!" Fortunately, the officer recognised him and calmly replied, "Behave yourself Barrington Levy". We arrived backstage and began acclimatising to the surroundings. It was incredibly dark and we were still adjusting our focus when all of a sudden, a loud "BOOM!" went off behind us.

I felt my leg tremble but I held firm and glanced at Smiley who had the look of a man who'd just bucked his toe on the pavement, and hoped no one had noticed.

His heart had jumped just like mine but before we could regain composure, "BOOM!" and "BOOM!" again. Another few of them went off in quick succession until we had to get a grip and look behind us to see what was going on. We saw Barrington laughing uncontrollably as he indulged in some mischief making, and was letting off the loudest firecrackers that I had ever heard. I don't know if you've ever heard the loudness of the firecrackers they use in Jamaica, but I can tell you England's bangers sound like hand claps by comparison. Still, we saw the funny side and in fact were somewhat relieved that it was a prank, and not a diss.

The Sunsplash show itself was fantastic and it was a special moment for us to see our UK compatriots Maxi Priest, Tippa Irie and Pato Banton take the stage by storm. With the energy that came from their performance we could imagine what it was going to be like for us too - Smiley and Asher on a stage in Jamaica! In the meantime, we met so many reggae stars who'd we heard about previously.

We'd raved to their music and even chatted on the instrumental versions of their records. We linked with stars like Big Youth and Sugar Minott, and others who were very popular at the time like Half Pint, Pinchers and Peter Metro. In fact, Metro and the English DJ Dominic stayed in our hotel in Mo'bay before making their long trek to town. That night was full of reasoning about reggae, MCs and the music business, and it was stimulating to hear Peter Metro's personal views on things.

It wasn't just music stars we met either, because we also met a few police stars like Isaiah Laing and Schoolboy Ritchie; two undercover Jamaican police who carried Third World Cop style reputations. People warned us to be careful of these police but that didn't deter Smiley in the slightest. The rumour was that Laing had already killed fifty-one people and this kept us aware, but not afraid of him. He invited us to a dance and we were kicking back in our hotel room with some locals when his driver arrived. Now we were cool until these locals began to question the guy picking us up as to whether he really worked with Laing, because they hadn't seen him before. This obviously made us slightly suspicious of the man.

While driving to the dance he turned into a gully, claiming that he was going to pick up the reggae artist Junior Demus. I hadn't heard what he'd been saying at first, and had to ask Smiley what was happening. Instinctively, we sat to attention in the darkness and went totally quiet. It wasn't worth looking around to keep watch because it was just so dark.

I could just about see my own hands, much less anything else, so all we could do was have faith, despite the fact it was the perfect setting for a slasher type horror movie – think a tropical version of Hostel One and Two. In a flash, I remembered how much gold we were wearing and in a panicky voice said to Smiley, 'they're coming. They're coming now'. Smiley frantically turned his head from left to right saying, "Where? Where?" We waited in anticipation and after another five minutes or so the driver got back in the car. This time I actually heard him say, "Him no deh ya".

Smiley and I spoke about this moment and always wondered if our panic attack was necessary or not. Still, it became one of our reference points whenever we debated overcoming our fears.

When we arrived at the dance Laing greeted us and told someone to usher us to our raving area. People were coming up to us all the time to talk to us, but none more so than one annoying brother in particular, who eventually received a hard box slap from one of the people Laing had assigned to us, warning him to stay away.

It seemed that Laing liked our company and he began to check us at the hotel quite regularly. He would adopt a routine when he came into our suite, put his gun on the side table, kick back on my bed and command, "order some room service nuh!" He and Schoolboy Ritchie took us on sightseeing trips and showed us a lot of the island. At one point we passed an area in the countryside where I thought I could smell ganja in a big way.

I whispered to Smiley in the back of the car and he could smell it too, but we never mentioned anything until later when we returned past the area. I asked Laing and Schoolboy if they could smell ganja and they instantly replied, "Yes, we raid round here a few times already but can never find anything." This led Smiley to proclaim, "These ganja man dem are clever!" We were both inspired by the things we saw, and the different ways of life.

Kingston Hot

Our time in Jamaica taught us so much, especially in terms of seeing people's raw drive and determination, even though they were in real need. It was as if we couldn't get enough of Jamaica on that first trip and so Smiley said we would have to come back real quick. Real quick to Smiley meant in two weeks' time and I was happy to return with him. I insisted this time that we travel in business-class as the seats in economy were too small and gave me backache. Smiley didn't hesitate and said, "business-class it is!"

We'd been so moved by some of the Jamaican people's plight, that we made sure to carry bags of clothes and items for the people we'd met and their families on our next trip there. This time we were accompanied by Blacker Dread from Sir Coxsone sound as he'd offered to link us up with the music producer Fatis from Exterminator Records – a label that boasted the services of reggae stars like the great Jamaican singing sensation Sanchez. Now the first mix-up of this journey happened when we were on the plane and about three quarters of the way to Jamaica when a flight attendant told Blacker that they'd been receiving complaints about the loudness of his music.

Blacker refused to turn down his ghetto blaster and even slapped the steward's wrist when he tried to turn the volume down. Oh, that made him angry alright! The steward threatened to have Blacker arrested when we got to Jamaica but that still never frightened Blacker one bit, and he continued to entertain us for the rest of our journey. For whatever reason, the steward never pursued his threat and we landed in Kingston without any further disturbances.

Leaving the plane in Kingston, we were overwhelmed again by the heat and overcrowding while waiting in line to pass through customs. Luckily, this time we were rescued by John Barnes, the famous footballer who was kind enough to tell the army security who came to collect him to let us through with him, which meant we fortunately avoided the long, long wait. Blacker had a man waiting for us outside the airport and he dropped us right back at the Wyndham Hotel. Now this stay turned out to be quite different to our first visit but it was just as exciting. We rolled with Fatis and encountered a different perspective to life in Jamaica, since Fatis wasn't exactly a people-pleaser.

People would shout out his name in respect as we drove past, but Fatis would callously respond with comments such as, "You know me, pussy hole?" I remember saying to Smiley that I hope we didn't see any of those guys when we weren't with Fatis. Smiley wasn't bothered and already seemed well in the spirit of things as he simply replied, "Fuck them!"

If we thought Barrington drove a bit crazily, it was really brought home to us when Fatis drove us to the top of Red Hills Road. Before the journey, Blacker and Smiley argued between them about who should ride shotgun up front, with Smiley winning, but before the journey back down the two of them fought to ride in the back because of the way Fatis drove on the way up! Fatis drove so fast up this little winding, cliff-top road that our hearts were in our mouths. It made us shudder with fear to think how he would be driving on the way back down.

Blacker won the fight for the back seat, as he said that everyone should stick to their original seats but the drive back down turned out to be comparatively tame as Fatis drove responsibly, knowing the real dangers and consequences that could easily happen from speeding down this dangerous hill.

Fatis was undoubtedly king of his realm and without much ado wanted us to know this. It seemed like he knew everyone and everyone knew him. The thing about Jamaica is that everything is tightly-knit, and everybody who is anybody tends to know anybody who is somebody, so it's always more than likely that people from completely different walks of life will cross paths at some stage. Now Fatis and Detective Laing were from the two different sides of life's road. Both were well-known figures and skilled specialists in their professions and yes, it would so happen that we fell in the middle of one of their path crossings. I won't go into detail but let's just say that if the risk factor was measured in terms of an earthquake, it would have easily registered as a 7.0 on the Richter scale. While Smiley, Blacker and I were bu'nin' some high-grade sensimilla in our hotel room and buzzing seriously, it didn't take too long before our part in the Laing and Fatis affair came into the conversation. Under the sensimilla buzz, someone mentioned how Laing had killed fifty-one people already. I looked at Smiley with a threatening stare and said, 'Smiley, that makes you fifty-two'. Lyrically sharp as ever he hit back with, "Asher, that makes you fifty-three." And then we both turned to Blacker in unison and joked, "Blacker, that makes you fifty four".

It wasn't the time for humour but the expression on Blacker's face, which let us know that he was in no way amused, lit the funny fuse. Smiley and I laughed until we were in hysterics, with eyes watering and stomachs paining. Every time we looked up at Blacker and saw him staring at us as if to say "you fools," this only made it worse and it became even harder for us to stop laughing. That good Jamaican sensimilla blew our minds to the point of extreme carelessness, and Blacker must have thought we were dangerously stupid. He thought we didn't realise the seriousness of our situation but that wasn't the case. We were aware of the dangers – we just couldn't stop laughing. The only thing that eventually stopped us was when the sensimilla's knockout effect came into play. We were out in a flash, our spliffs unfinished and hitched in the ashtrays, all of us resembling babies who'd fallen asleep long before finishing their milk. Quick rhyme of advice: *"Be careful my friend whenever you bu'n - the sensi in that Jamaican sun - remember at first it might be fun - but all of a sudden you're finished and done"*. The mix up was soon resolved and we left Jamaica with wonderful stories to tell and great memories to hold onto. I have to state that writing this part right now and recalling these memories makes me feel Smiley's presence in a big way.

By the mid 1980's the music scene was rapidly changing and record labels began to pump more money into filming videos to promote their artists. A moderate song accompanied by a creative video could increase record sales tenfold. To cater for this demand a new 24-hour music station, MTV, had recently launched in America. Initially MTV would only air the music of white pop and rock acts on its rotation playlist. Ironically, the first black band MTV allowed on its main playlist was the Birmingham reggae act Musical Youth with 'Pass the Dutchie' – I guess because they were seen as quirky, non-threatening British kids. Although Michael Jackson's 'Billie Jean' video is credited with spreading the popularity of MTV, the station witnessed its greatest growth when it aired the videos of hip-hop MCs like Run DMC, The Beastie Boys and LL Cool J. This was the era of the microphone - the DJs and MCs. You didn't have to be blessed with a velvet-toned voice, or spend years perfecting your pitch. You just needed some good lyrics, a microphone and an attitude.

Our popularity saw to it that we received scores of offers to perform in different countries, although some never happened because of promoters' disorganisation and lack of planning.

Kingston Hot

One offer that Smiley and I did choose to accept was from a promoter called Johnny, who wanted us to tour America alongside other talented UK artists such as Leslie Lyrics, Lorna G and Cinderella.

Chapter 13

Empire State Of Rhymes

Why we chose to go with this promoter when he didn't even have the money for our advance mystifies me even now, but the energy at the time meant that we rolled with the risk. Our troubles began right from the start after we'd waited for hours at New Jersey airport for the supposed pick-up driver who never arrived, and then had to take the bus to our destination. Our next complaint was about the actual place where the promoter wanted us to stay – a small, small, small room in an elder woman's little, little, little flat. Smiley wasn't having this so we immediately checked into a hotel off the Belt Park Way, and insisted the promoter would have to refund us. It didn't take too long before we were introduced to the seriousness of the area. The first cab we took, the driver stated right away that he wouldn't be going anywhere with us wearing all that gold, since it would get us all killed. Bowing to his superior knowledge of the locality, we tucked in our chains to ease his concerns and encouraged him to carry on. These first warnings - being stood up at the airport, riding on a bus with our luggage and nearly being shacked with Old Mother Hubbard, hinted that we were already swimming against the tide.

This was old New York, the murder capital of the Western world. The news broadcasts we were seeing on television remained inadvertently in our subconscious and would prove to start affecting our judgement. Broadcasts such as "A man was shot and killed today for taking someone's parking space" and "A man was shot and killed today for taking too long in the phone booth" entitled us to be fully on guard as we became accustomed to the US lifestyle. The entire outlook was grim but the ambiguity of proceedings still brought an air of excitement, and that urged us to live in the moment. The fact was we were already there and so we decided to live by the motto, "The show must go on". While we were waiting for the day of the first show, the five of us decided to take a cab to a nearby record shop. On arrival at the shop the cab driver told us the fare would be five dollars. Smiley believed this was overpriced, and so he gave Lorna G three dollars to give him. The cab driver blew his top like an olden day kettle and snarled, "That's why I don't take Jamaicans!" Then he tore up the money and threw it on the floor. His irascible reaction corresponded with the entire cowboy attitude we were encountering and so we thought, 'Maybe we shouldn't stay too long at the record shop in case he comes back with an Uzi or something just as lethal'.

The night before our first show we went to a club called Reggae Lounge in Manhattan. We'll later find out that this is the only promotion that was done for the whole tour. The word we received about the Reggae Lounge was that it was the home club for many reggae artists from Jamaica. It was the venue for the ballers, big spenders and no doubt real gangsters.

It was a sizeable venue, holding approximately 800 to 1000 people and as per norm it was full. The five of us arrived accompanied by the promoter and immediately my attention was drawn to the metal detector at the door. In England the only places you would find metal detectors were airports, government buildings and royal courts, so once more we were reminded of the seriousness of America. Sadly, the night before there had been a gangland shootout at a nearby club that saw five people killed, and so it was to no surprise to see the security guards on full alert. The Jamaican reggae DJ Louis Ranking hosted for the evening and his stage personality was no different to the gangster character that he played in the movie Third World Cop. He stopped the music and in his personal hard-hearted tone, made a statement about the killings that had happened the night before.

It went something in the way of, "You see last night whe dem kill the people dem and gwan like a so it go? Mek me tell you something, if a bwoy ever t'ink say him can do that ya so him would get a big dutty surprise. ME NO RAMP WID PEOPLE SO IF A BWOY T'INK DEM BAD AND WANT SHOOT SOMEBODY – COME SHOOT ME!"

As I surveyed the club to see the people's reactions, I caught a glimpse of Smiley doing exactly the same. Some people were smiling and some were actually laughing but the majority of the people held serious expressions on their faces. We were still commenting on Louis Ranking's statement and the people's reactions when our promoter broke the news that two out of the five of us were requested to perform on stage. Smiley and I happily offered each other the opportunity to go on stage alongside Louis Ranking but eventually I took the responsibility and obliged.

Lorna G and I made our way to the stage area and were greeted by Louis Ranking with a respectful but brusque manner. "Yes, tell me when you ready, seen?" Lorna G went on first and performed her lyrics 'Triple The Condom' that tore down the dance as the people warmed to her easily.

Then it was my turn. I was still in contention with myself as to which lyrics I would deliver. I took the mic, approached the front of the stage and automatically chat my lyrics 'Hustlers In Jamaica'. The reaction from the crowd was good, but the greatest satisfaction was when Louis Ranking said on the mic afterwards, "Wait, why nobody never tell me say this DJ so bad (good)? If mi did ever know me woulda bring him in much more proper from start!" I found it heartening and when I returned to our corner in the venue, Smiley was the first to congratulate me on my performance. The next night, the first show of the tour was in the Bronx, but because there was no actual promotion done we ended up having to manage the door entrance ourselves while hoping that people would come. It was a miserable night as hardly anyone came at all and to round it off we had to defend Cinderella at the end of the dance when some local youths threw bottles at her outside the club because she wouldn't talk to them. The next show was to be held in Brooklyn but again due to the lack of promotion the show was cancelled and instead we flew on a "blow all over the place" miniature plane to Boston. This Tonka plane only had seats on one side and the aisle on the other.

It felt like we had no engine and were directed by the winds... It was a sure test of character for anyone who flew on that thing. The show in Boston was where we came into our own, it was ram-packed and the crowd was highly appreciative of our lyrics. Smiley performed 'Police Officer' and a range of lyrics from his catalogue; I performed 'Hustlers In Jamaica' again backed up with a barrage of lyrics and Leslie, Lorna and Cinderella rocked the dance with their waves of styles and lyrics. The excellence of this dance in Boston made up for all the niggling problems that were threatening to spoil the rest of the tour, and will remain in our memory banks for a long time.

There was still enough time left for more dramas to happen. One time Leslie got so angry with Smiley in New York that he stormed out of a cab and we never saw him again until we returned to England. Leslie said he was totally frustrated with Culture's spoilt behaviour but the good thing was that they were absolutely fine with each other back in London. Another drama that happened was arguably the worst moment of the whole tour. We were waiting for a cab in the foyer of our hotel, which was located somewhere off the Belt Park Way.

I was speaking to Smiley in a Jamaican accent about how well the dance in Boston went when a white, short, very skinny and raggedy youth who was sitting in the reception area became very agitated and suddenly stormed out of the hotel while cursing foul language. Because of all the little dramas that were happening throughout the tour, I automatically said to Smiley that he'd probably gone for his gun. I wasn't too far off as it happened because he rushed back in – not with a gun like I predicted, but a long, rusty sword that he waved menacingly at us. He came right up to my face saying things in his strong American accent like, "What you saying now, mother fucker?" and "I'm gonna fuck you up". I asked him what his problem was but his main reply was that he just didn't like me. My response was to stand as close to him as possible so he wouldn't be able to get a good swing at me with the sword, and to keep telling him to relax. A mature woman who worked in the hotel came into reception and asked us what the matter was and with that, this nutty youth stormed out of the hotel again. It turned out that this woman was his mother and he'd come to pick her up, but to us the only explanation we could find for his mad behaviour was that he obviously had a drugs problem or something.

He was crazily intimidated by our differences and maybe he just didn't like the Jamaican accent I'd been speaking in. Whatever it was, I wouldn't have let that little shit get the better of me. Even with his weapon I would have beaten him until I was tired like when Blacker and the Coxsone crew beat up a radio DJ one time for playing the Saxon side of a tape on the radio and not the Coxsone side. They got so tired beating him, they were actually out of breath and I could actually imagine myself similarly running out of breath while beating this foolish boy. That situation in the US and the few other bugging issues that happened meant we stayed completely on our guard at all times. To be honest I'd actually forgotten about that tour until recently when I was searching on YouTube and trying to find an old track when I came across a post called Reggae English Invasion and thought I'd watch it. To my total surprise I saw Leslie Lyrics, then me and then Smiley. The video clip is around 12 minutes long and I sat there almost all the way through trying to work out where in England this dance could have been filmed, then I heard "Big up all the people from Boston". That brought the memories flooding back, and I instantly began to write this part of Smiley's life so I could include it in the book.

Chapter 14

Joyride

By 1989 the takeover was complete. Hip-hop had become the dominant music force and MCs were kings. Rap music outsold everything and MCs were shaping the cultural landscape of not only America, but also the world. When Run DMC teamed up with Aerosmith for 'Walk This Way' this was the handover, and the baton had passed from rock to rap.

Smiley and I went to see Run DMC when they first came to Brixton. In fact we saw most of the early US hip-hop acts and noticed it was mostly the same crowd that had been following us for years, but they'd switched their allegiance from reggae to hip-hop. These hip-hop guys were tightly managed, had sponsorship deals and it was evident from their stage shows that they had solid financial backing. Did we miss a trick? Did we peak too early in our careers?

Smiley's nephew Merlin had followed his uncle's footsteps and became an MC. Merlin's breakout hit 'Who's in the House' featured the Beatmasters and was a take on Run- DMC's 'Who's House'. It was a pleasure to see Smiley gamble on Merlin in a different way when he was given a short-term jail sentence.

Joyride

'Who's In The House' was riding high in the national charts at the time but the bird that Merlin was doing made it impossible for him to perform it on Top Of The Pops. Smiley, typically, took the "im" off impossible and used his status, character and charm to make it possible. First he called the prison and asked to speak to the governor. "You alright gov?" was his introduction when the governor came on the line, and "I'm Smiley Culture" was obviously next. Somehow, he persuaded the governor into agreeing to release Merlin from the prison for one day to appear on Top Of The Pops, which in my world of experience is unprecedented. I don't know about you but I have never heard of anything like it – a prisoner being allowed out of prison to do a performance on television?

Maybe I'm late in the day and it happens all of the time, but I remember some of my friends who were serving jail sentences not even being allowed out to attend family funerals, much less perform on television but Smiley had done it again – he'd defied the odds and made history. His adrenaline level must have been at full capacity that day as he endeavoured to make it an unforgettable experience. He said, "Seny we have to pick him up in style".

He requested my driving license and ordered the highest specked Mercedes Benz in Hertz's rental car showroom, in Edgware Road. The burgundy coloured E600, top-of-the-range Benz was a driver's dream, and I loved driving it. In fact we both loved the drive and profile so much that when Smiley decided that we should keep it for a while longer after Merlin's big day, I happily agreed. Man, we pulled up outside that prison looking like rich kids, and when the guards opened the prison gates to let us drive onto the prison grounds it was like we were royalty. The prisoners who could see us from their windows were cheering frantically in such a manner I wondered if it was because they recognised us, or if they'd just received word their paroles had come through. Merlin stepped out to a reception of more cheers and as he entered the car I could see he was in awe of the situation. It was his moment; we agreed with the governor to return him by 9 pm and made off to enjoy the day.

Top Of The Pops was always filmed two days before it was to be aired and the artists were required to attend three rehearsals throughout the day before they could perform later, at around 7 pm.

Joyride

The first rehearsal was early morning for a sound check; the second around mid-afternoon for a visual check and the third was early evening for the actual dress rehearsal. That meant we had to be there early in the morning and it left Smiley very little time to get Merlin some new clothes. We hurriedly kitted out Merlin and arrived at Top Of The Pops more or less on time.

Merlin graced the stage like a bird gliding across water when hunting its prey and he commanded his zone like a lion dominating its territory. This US style of rap flow was captivating a new English audience and gave some much-needed impetus to the UK rap scene. However, when it was time for us to make our way back to the prison we realised that time was against us. I drove as fast as possible so we would live up to our word and more importantly, not land Merlin in trouble with the prison governor. We got him there just after the given time, but there was no need to worry as the governor was happy and said he was looking forward to watching Merlin on TV.

Smiley asked me to drop him home and said I should keep the car until we linked the next day. We could then decide on how long we should keep it.

The payments for the car was originally coming from Smiley's account but after the first month of us driving and posing all over London and he received the first bill of £2,000, he decided to find someone else to start covering the costs.

The chosen one was Ken Hinds. Somehow Smiley painted a picture of the benefits he would gain in the future by investing his money now. It literally took three months before Ken put paid to Smiley's promises and cancelled his credit card payments with the rental car company. It was somewhat hurtful to me that my publishing advance was the means by which we paid Ken back - £6,000 from my first real healthy advance was gone just like that, but the show had to go on.

Smiley searched for another sponsor and found one in the form of Ron, the exhaust fitter at our local car garage. Jamaican Ron was a lovely man and always helped us with our cars but this was another level all together. No matter though, Ron gave his credit card details and became rental car sponsor number two. A month later, Ron began to ring Smiley I would say occasionally, but after the second month had passed, occasionally became frequently and by the coming of the end of the third month frequently became twenty times a day.

Smiley would answer sometimes and reassure him that his money was safe but most of the time he dodged the calls and told people to tell him he wasn't about. Still, to keep Ron sweet, Smiley would pop in from time to time and tell him a magnificent story that ensured we were given more time with the car.

So many months had passed until instead of the car being a luxury for us it was now a burden, and I didn't like the way things were looking at all. Yes, I drove it most of the time but most of that time it was on Smiley's runnings, and yes I kept it clean as if it was my own car but that's just the way Mum brought me up. "Cleanliness is Godliness" was one of her regular sayings. As it was my driver's licence used in the initial renting of the car, it was me who would face any consequences. The rental company was now contacting me with threats insisting that if they didn't get their car back by the end of the month they would cancel the agreement and report the car stolen. It became the car that we didn't like anymore and we both tried to dodge the responsibility like kids who broke something of their parents and preferred to hide it, oblivious to the fact that it could bring us more trouble in the long run.

Joyride

After finishing our day I would drive to my home first so that the car could stay in Smiley's possession and he did the same to me. We both pulled every stop out of our boxes of tricks to ensure that neither of us would be the one held liable for the car, or the ginormous bill that had accrued. Eventually, the rental car company gave us a specific time to bring the car back and we quickly conformed. Everyone in the Hertz office looked at us as if we were crazy, knowing what kind of money had been wasted on that car. Months had passed and by now the bill was almost £10,000. Ron, in particular, wanted payback. At least £4,000 was taken from his credit card and because he saw more of me than Smiley, it was me who took the brunt of his wrath. Even brothers, much less friends, would have become enemies for less than that in our world. But Ron is a good man and he took it with a pinch of salt.

He knew all about Smiley and certainly admired his "high to the sky" personality. Smiley maintained his friendly reasoning with Ron while slowly but surely paying back the money over a period of time. No matter the weather, Smiley always went to great lengths to ensure that we maintained top status.

Joyride

The car showroom people told him that it would be much cheaper to buy two cars on monthly finance packages and so he instinctively bought two C-Class Mercedes for us. Mine was burgundy-coloured with a beige interior while his was white with a black interior and kitted with a full complement of spoilers. I feel obliged to mention that it was my lyrics that actually justified Smiley's payment for mine. Smiley was offered the opportunity to return to America to record an album produced by Run DMC. However, when it came closer to the time he told me that he didn't have any new lyrics written, and asked if he could take some of mine. He knew I was always writing lyrics and he probably gambled on this should it be needed.

We sat down in my flat in Notre Dame Estate and went through some of my lyrics on tape. "That one... that one... and that one," he said, as he chose lyrics after lyrics. Now I still believed that I'd get my big hit record one-day and so I said no to some of the lyrics, because I wanted to use them for myself. Yet still I gave him about ten different lyrical styles and he went to America well equipped.

Joyride

I gave him lyrics such as 'What Have I Done?' which was an answer to Janet Jackson's hit song 'What Have You Done For Me Lately?' and 'Flashback To The Vietnam War' which was a historically factual piece on events during that war. Out of the lyrics, the record company chose around seven to be featured on the album including one called 'Can't Stop The Rap', which was chosen as the single. Looking back at it now, I can only imagine what was going through Smiley's mind before plucking up the courage to ask me for my lyrics. Working with Run DMC could have elevated him to another level, and so it was an honour to help him out with the lyrics.

Smiley, Mikey and Fox went to America and I stayed to manage the studio in New Cross. He called every day and we kept each other thoroughly informed of all developments. One day he'd gone with Run DMC to pick up their new car from the showroom and they paid for it in cash. He was amazed that when the car salesman told them the number plates weren't ready, Run DMC took one of the car dealership's number plates, put it in the window of the car and took the car anyway. He also said that he'd heard of a man who was big in the music business called Danny Sims, and wanted to link him.

He said the only thing is; everyone he asks about Danny says that he's not someone to mess around with. I imagine by now you should know at least a little bit about Smiley's character to know that he made sure to find him and get in contact. Danny was an elder man in his early 60s, but he was stronger than an ox. He was a tall, impressive man with a voice of rock-stone, and he commanded respect when he spoke.

Danny is credited with discovering Bob Marley and Peter Tosh. He signed them to their first publishing deal and then sold the contract to Chris Blackwell. Danny was a symbol of success and that was the only thing Smiley was concerned with. He saw how Sims lived in a Manhattan mansion serviced by butlers and maids, and was married to Beverly Johnson, America's first black supermodel. The pair took to each other immediately and formed a bond in friendship and business so tight that Smiley told people Danny was his uncle and Danny told people that Smiley was his nephew.

In 1990, Danny and Smiley secured a deal with a publishing company in Edgware Road for us to run a record label called WAM Records, which stood for World Artist Management, or "What A Mess" as some described it.

Joyride

Two Jewish businessmen, Saul and Ruben, were co-directors of the publishing company and happy to establish the record label with Danny and Smiley. This partnership seemed good at first, but as time progressed we began to witness the cracks in Saul and Ruben's business relationship.

These disruptions became so regular that it was apparent that sooner or later the label would suffer the consequences. It was mayhem as they battled each other like enemies. It got so bad that when one of them agreed something the other would disagree, and when one of them promised to take care of something the other would do it first, out of spite. This made it more difficult for us to deliver any meaningful product but taking everything else into consideration, this would still be a memorable chapter in our lives. Smiley made sure the label not only signed international artists, but also gave some of our local talent an opportunity to record their music. WAM signed Mannix and Fox, who received £400 per month each, whilst I received £800 per month. Artists such as Jocelyn Brown and Oliver Cheatham, and producers like Ricky Rainbow and Mike Barnes were flown in from America to work with us, with all their expenses being paid for by the company.

Working with them, together with our monthly wage, made it really an enjoyable time. We recorded tracks that most people thought were hit songs but circumstances beyond our control ensured that no tracks were officially released to the wider public. I tried to make things happen for myself, like pressing up a few white labels of various tracks and plugging them on the radio, but we couldn't seem to get past the starting line. Nevertheless the music we made kept us inspired and some of the people we brought in became very close to us, like Madla from North London.

We were judging a singing and DJ competition in north London when a competitor approached us. We couldn't believe what we were hearing as this young man pleaded with us to let him win. He went on and on and returned to plead again at every given opportunity. It was Madla, and that was the beginning of our acquaintance. Madla was a short, small-framed and dark-skinned young man, and the joker in our pack. He always made us laugh, even when our moods weren't good. Sometimes Smiley would be in a serious mood but Madla would spontaneously say joke after joke until Smiley would eventually burst out laughing.

Joyride

The distance that he lived from us would be a chore for most people but he made the journey from north to south London simplicity itself. For a sustained period of time he rolled with us every day and it even got to the stage where he would pack his necessities to stay over. Madla's humorous and compulsive personality was infectious and even when situations were dire he still had the tendency to make everyone laugh. He made situations seem nowhere as bad as they were. It really didn't matter to him. He was on a comedy planet and didn't care who he annoyed. He joked about anything at any time until eventually we not only became accustomed to his jokes, but found that we were also reliant on them. When Smiley's girlfriend walked out in a huff one day, Madla joked in a Bajan accent, "Boy, you better run after she and say sorry Smiley!" Even the time when Smiley slammed down the phone after losing a music deal, Madla waited for him to cool down from his rant and then jokingly asked in that same Bajan accent, "Do you think he did like it when you cuss him out Smiley?"

For some reason, it was very quiet and tense in the car one midweek evening. Smiley was driving quite fast in and out of the traffic on our way back from Harlesden.

Madla was in the back of the car while I was in the passenger seat wondering why Smiley was driving in such a manner. Madla suddenly croaked in an elderly tone, "Smiley why you driving so erratic boy?" We all burst into laughter and the tension was cleared. Madla's gift of random comedy was certainly one of the bright spots in the ups and downs of our joy ride.

Smiley, however, was concentrating more on the business side, and working on major deals with record companies. The record label that we'd formed in Edgware Road lasted for about a year until Saul and Ruben handed Danny and Smiley a bill for around £400,000. The two of them were fuming at receiving it and when the record label finally folded, Smiley turned the tables and insisted that Saul and Ruben owed him for all the time he was there.

They were more than reluctant to give Smiley any money and made it as difficult as they could to avoid paying him anything, but eventually they agreed to meet with him at their offices in Edgware Road. We went for the meeting and they took us into one of their offices on the first floor.

Joyride

The meeting started off well but as time progressed, frustration started to kick in on both sides and the verbal exchanges became heated. Smiley was insisting they paid him £100,000 in wages and produced documented evidence to support his demands. Saul and Ruben, unusually in agreement, paid the documentation no mind and refused to release any money whatsoever as they said they could not find any logic in the claim that they owed him. While all these verbal exchanges were in full swing we suddenly heard the sound of police radios. Saul and Ruben had somehow got a message out to call the police, who came straight to the office and told us to leave the premises immediately. Outside in the hallway, Smiley turned to test one of the officer's resolve. "Do you know who I am mate?" he asked. The officer replied yes and taking the initiative, Smiley continued. "Look, I've been working for these guys for a year and they don't want to pay me my wages of £100,000". "In that case, I'll give you another twenty minutes," said the officer before pointing to his badge and saying, "There's my number. I work over the road at Edgware Road police station, so when you get paid make sure you pay me a visit". The look on Saul and Ruben's faces when we went back to their office was a sight to remember.

Their expressions of disbelief were soon followed by their humble agreement to pay Smiley £70,000, together with the return of all the recordings that we'd made there. From his experience at Fashion Records, Smiley had learned that verbal contracts are only good if both parties stand by them, and that a promise is comfort to a fool. The only promise Smiley believed in was the declaration on paper money. "I promise to pay the bearer on demand the sum of..."

As time went on this became a pattern, and he did deal after deal with record companies but whenever one got on the wrong side of him, he'd definitely let them know about it. It soon became impossible for Smiley to do business with certain record companies and so he'd send in other people instead, telling them not to mention his name.

In the mid-90s a young man from Leicester paid him a visit at my flat, and brought him a tape of an R & B singer who was also from Leicester. Smiley hooked him up with Danny Sims and said that he'd take his percentage when things happened for the artist. Things did happen for the artist. He got hit songs throughout Europe and his breakout single reached No. 2 in the US Billboard chart.

He became a superstar, just as Smiley had predicted, so now it was time for him to collect his percentage according to what they'd agreed. However, when Smiley's demand was made clear, the artist wasn't happy and tried in almost every way possible to get out of paying him any money. Smiley turned the heat on and this artist tried increasingly desperate avoidance tactics. We were chilling at Smiley's house in Streatham once when one of the artist's friends rang him. This guy sounded hysterical on the phone as he announced that the artist had died in a car crash. They wanted to convince Smiley of this so much that they'd even contacted the newspapers. Smiley refused to believe it, went to the artist's house later that night and found him at home with "his feet up, kicking the beat up". The artist was so shocked that all he could say was the phrase, "Niggas in my yard". What a phrase! We couldn't help using it ourselves on numerous occasions, because of the way it rolled off the tongue. "Niggas in my yard..." The bobbing and weaving went on for some time until it got to the stage where Smiley visited the artist's management office. He must have made a significant impression because the next day he got his payment of around £130,000, although the actual amount would change whenever Smiley recalled the tale.

When news of this leaked in the ghetto, a few people were upset. They thought that because Smiley had used their names as leverage in his negotiations, this warranted a slice of the money. Yard Man Del and Little Andy rushed Smiley in Brixton and gave him a real shake-up, yet he still never gave a penny to them. He did though, call the guy who originally brought down the tape of the artist and they again met at my flat, where Smiley gave him a shoebox full of money that I presume came from the payment he'd received from the artist.

Despite all these goings-on, Smiley's house in Streatham still holds some good memories for me. Our vibes were certainly at amazing heights when we were recording in the studio there. We had the honour of recording the former undisputed world heavyweight boxing champion Lennox Lewis, and it was something else watching him perform the lyrics that Fox had written for him.

Lennox tried his best to deliver the lyrics that went, "I'm on a mission – to seek and destroy.
"I came up from the ghetto, I ain't no boy.
One man, one goal, one destiny.
That's the vibe that I keep within me.

Contact sport was the thing for me,
And boxing suited me down to the "T".
So I did it, got with it, without a doubt.
Know what I mean – It's a knock out."

Unfortunately, things weren't as good as they seemed from the outside and the papered-over cracks were beginning to show. Smiley's attitude to making sure he paid his mortgage was becoming unbearable to the team and often hinted of desperation. We were all feeling the strain and even though we were struggling financially, we still did everything we could to help Smiley pay it. But eventually we reached a point of realisation. Mikey and Fox really had no other option but to leave and pursue their own destinies while I made my exit more subtly. I grew frustrated with the fact that our family bond, having been so strong for such a long time, was now threatened by financial pressures. We needed money yes, but this was turning into a fiasco as it meant all the money we made was going to Smiley's mortgage. He wasn't making money quick enough and his home and car bills were mounting up. Things were changing rapidly and it just didn't seem the same anymore.

Joyride

Smiley and Peter King had an irreparable fall-out over some deal, and I began opting out of a few situations myself. Although it felt like I was letting him down, I'm glad now that I stuck to my gut instinct. I knew that I had to break away from the deteriorating vibes that were taking us over, and so it was only a matter of time before I started to do my own thing entirely. That was when our close bond certainly tapered, although the spiritual understanding between us remained strong. Madla opted to operate with me and even though I was in temporary accommodation in East Dulwich, he and Peter King visited me all the time.

I tried to mend the situation with King and Smiley a few times but to no avail. Fortunately, Smiley and I still spoke on the phone a lot and continued visiting each other without any fuss. Eventually though, both the house in Streatham and his car were repossessed. This was a particularly hard time for him and his disappointment was clear for everyone to see. He was in a foul and miserable mood and it felt as if he was blaming us for his ill fortunes. He'd never have a smile on his face as he entered my flat on Acre Lane but he was always respectful as we greeted each other.

Joyride

He spent considerable time in deep thought and mainly spoke in little bursts about how he needed to make money, and fast. I let him store some of his furniture and equipment at my flat and offered him the opportunity to stay most of the time. Smiley of course, wasn't going to let the situation get the better of him and he wrestled with the elements of life to rise up again. He bought a Rolls Royce as retail therapy, albeit a very old one, and went on a shopping spree to purchase a whole range of designer wear.

He fought through the bad and emerged with a new energy that would see him start moving to a higher standard of living once more. Things began to improve and when he got his house in Croydon, he collected the furniture and equipment that he'd stored at my flat and built another studio. That's where I recorded some memorable tracks with artists like Barry Boom and Carolene Thompson. Smiley insisted and ensured that the "joyride" continued and decided to take a crew of around thirteen to MIDEM, the annual music industry event in Cannes. I went along for that one and experienced the new, exuberant Smiley, who was constantly pumped and keeping things upbeat in terms of behaviour, attitude and ego.

Joyride

His girlfriend at the time made the trip with us and I must admit that she did well to absorb Smiley's contrary attitude towards her in front of us all. But her worries were just a drop in the ocean compared to the level of intensity Smiley put into his efforts to let other people know who was boss. The trip began nicely enough as he hired two Mercedes A-Class cars for us to travel in, but soon after that, the dramas began. Smiley chose to drive one of the cars himself whilst Lloydie Crucial, an artist who was based in Harlesden, drove the other. I travelled with Lloydie and while we were on the roads I kept in close contact with Smiley via Walkie-talkie, it was like some real private eye shit. Now the speed at which Smiley drove along the freeway in Cannes was unimaginably fast and Lloydie made sure that he stayed right on his tail. Both showed little care about possible consequences.

The first incident happened after a hotel manager decided to block an area in the hotel where we'd raved and entertained people the day before. We'd had so much fun and the coup was that Smiley had bought most of the champagne from external outlets. We'd sneaked them into the hotel's event area and only bought maybe one or two bottles from the hotel bar itself.

The manager had caught on to this and by the next day was totally prepared for us. He blocked the area where we had previously jammed with a whole load of tables and chairs, while a rope hung across the area with a sign stating 'RESERVED'. He made it his duty to confront us, "You are not welcome here", he blazed up, kind of like Marlon Brando in the Godfather movie. He actually resembled a gangster in the way he and his security ushered us off the premises. We left peacefully, but, little did he know, and nor did any of us as a matter of fact, that Smiley was determined to see this man before we left Cannes.

In the meantime we found another location to do our thing, and ended up partying with another former heavyweight champion, Evander Holyfield. This little club in the suburbs of nowhere had ran out of champagne and so courtesy of Smiley Culture's secret stash, Evander was able to continue happily with his entertainment. More disturbingly for our team was the fact that our smoke was all but finished and so we decided to see if we could get some locally. It was around 2. 30am and I had agreed to go on the journey to pick up some herbs that a French guy in the club had told us about.

Joyride

Smiley stayed in the club with Evander while I rolled with the French guy, Lloydie the driver, and a couple of others from our team. The French guy directed us to an estate that was around 15 minutes drive away, where we saw two youths chilling. The French guy translated for us, asked if they could assist us and the two youths went away leaving us wondering if they were going to return. They did return, but without any exaggeration they were now with a posse of at least another fifteen youths. How did they round up a posse this big at these hours of the morning? Where did that posse come from looking so 'up for it'? They must have been partying or hanging out in a 24-hour drug spot. Either way, they were too lively for the calm of the morn. Before we knew it they were positioned around the A Class and opening the doors while jargoning menacingly in French. One of the guys opened my door but I just grunted, 'Whe' you a do? MOVE', slammed back my door and said in a quite urgent tone to Lloydie, "Drive, drive, drive..." It wasn't good. In fact it was somewhat embarrassing for us when Lloydie did try to drive and found the automatic gearbox wasn't in gear. All we got was monster revving from the engine.

Joyride

Eventually Lloydie got the car into gear and we raced off like we were aiming for pole position in the French Grand Prix. On our return to the club we told Smiley what happened and he was totally bemused by the whole story, saying he didn't know whether to be vexed because we didn't get weed or because of the fact that we were chased.

He waited until the day we were to leave Cannes before orchestrating our next moves and driving to a spot in town where we could find some hustlers. We got out of the cars and Smiley called one of them over. "Acheter," he said, which in case you don't know means "buy" in French. The guy acted suspiciously as they do, and took us over to a less conspicuous area to show us his merchandise, as they do.

He handed over just the one bag but Smiley insisted that he wanted to buy everything the guy had and so he cautiously took out everything to show him. Suddenly he had the guy by the wrist and stunned everybody by saying, "You're under arrest". The guy looked at me with a real confused expression on his face, probably hoping that I'd say it's a joke, but all I could do was disguise my surprise by nodding at him, as if to confirm Smiley's statement.

Smiley then took the initiative by speaking into the Walkie-talkie to Donovan his son, who had the other handset across the road, saying, "We've got him, bring over the van..." The guy nearly dropped to the floor with disbelief but somehow he cleverly dragged his hand away in a desperate attempt to escape and ran as fast as he could through the nearby market.

We ran after him for a while yelling, "Police, stop him" but then turned back to go to our cars, laughing like mad. It was bordering on unbelievable that Smiley had pulled that stunt and it was even more remarkable that we got away with it. I don't think he'd actually known he was going to do that - it seemed entirely instinctive. Next, he had to take care of some unfinished business with the hotel manager, who Smiley believed had dissed him a measure too far.

Entering the hotel foyer, our man was sitting at a small table accompanied by a smartly dressed individual and looking as if he was conducting some serious business. Walking straight over to him, Smiley pointed at him and yelled, "YOU..." I don't know if this man was terribly frightened deep down, but on the surface he held his composure as Smiley laid into him with some ear-splitting, verbal abuse.

He gave him such a cussing that it would require regular counselling to recover from it. The man must still be having nightmares about some of the things that Smiley told him that day. The businessman sat next to him never said a word throughout what was easily a ten minute episode. Even when Smiley asked him if he was defending the guy, he still never moved or spoke. Smiley was so maddened by the manager's previous attitude towards him that he kept cussing him on our way out. Afterwards, feeling satisfied with the revenge he'd exacted he said calmly, "I think he got the message".

Once we'd returned to England it was back to our separate works for us, although we still called each other regularly. He moved to Warlingham, a middle-class suburb of Surrey, and spoke to me about the gold and diamond trade a lot. He was researching this in a big way, and after a time it became the main thing he talked about with real excitement. He clearly wanted me to get involved, but somehow I just didn't. Smiley would call me and be totally hyped up. He'd make it obvious that he was making big money, and held regular barbecues at his house. These were attended by a variety of people, from diplomats to business associates to family and friends.

Most of the time when I went to see him there were visitors at his house, many of whom I didn't even know. He'd introduce me as his old music and sparring partner, and would often recount an old-time music or war story. Long-standing friends would say to me on numerous occasions that they didn't like what was going on, and how he had a lot of hangers-on around him. Some of us even told Smiley to his face, warning him to be aware of all these new faces, but he always gave the impression that he was in control and had everything in perspective. I used to tell him about the difficulties I faced in my work and he'd say he knew exactly what I meant, which I took as a sign that he was going through similar problems with people who had hidden agendas. Smiley had a drinking habit by now and would drink brandy after brandy.

This concerned me considering that we were Ribena and sensimilla people, and used to fight against alcohol in our lyrics. He'd always say that he had it under control and could quit, and that he was going to quit drinking and smoking anytime soon. He was travelling a lot and always showing me magazines, documents and contracts with reference to his gold and diamond business.

Joyride

I remember him showing me a music contract that he'd received from a company for a million pounds, and telling me that they'd given him 50% in advance. After he bought a Bentley, he complained that the police were enquiring about it, but again he said he had everything under control. Then in the latter part of 2010, he called and asked me if I'd like to perform with him at a festival in Buckinghamshire. I agreed, and on the day of the show, I travelled in the Bentley with Smiley driving and radio DJ Gammo Speng in the back seat. There was an entourage of cars and a barrage of people that came along as well. Strangely for him, Smiley was very quiet on the way there, as if something was definitely bothering him. I thought maybe it was his girlfriend annoying him because I knew that always affected his attitude and mood but I didn't ask and really thought he would be okay. It was just odd that he was so hyped up not so long ago, and now he was so down. When I think about it now, I know he wanted to tell me something but for some reason he found it awkward to talk to me. Anyhow, the show was tremendous and I brought him onstage to an excellent reception. He performed his old hits and the crowd loved them, just as if they were recent.

332

On returning from the show, he was still in a downbeat mood and again I wondered what could possibly be wrong with him. Little was I to know that this show was to be our last together, and little did I know that Smiley's depressed persona was an indication of what seriousness lay ahead. One day while I was at work, I received a phone call from a friend who asked me if I had seen the Evening Standard. He said that I should get the paper because there was an article about Smiley in it. I read the article and was astounded. The headline stated that he was appearing in court facing cocaine charges. I rang Smiley immediately and asked him if it was true. He said yes, but everything was cool. Eventually he said he wanted to speak to me and when he came to see me, he told me what he was going through and how he was feeling. I was shocked and saddened for him, and angry about the fact that he said the police had never found any illegal substance on him but were connecting him through someone else. Smiley was going through one of his rough patches again and I tried to make him aware of this, while reminding him of how many times he'd risen up in his life. I reminded him about the times when we had nothing but our love of music, and how he'd carved out a career in the music industry.

Joyride

I reminded him of the fame, the adulation, the money, the bling and the cars, but most of all the dexterity he had to turn things back in his favour. From the moment we started making music, our journey had been a joy ride. Just one big joy ride...

Chapter 15

Nine Nights And A Funeral

We had to be the main attraction everywhere we went, and if we weren't, then Smiley would somehow see to it that it soon changed. When things were down he would always brighten things back up. He named himself "the Don" and one of his favourite sayings was, "Everybody have to come back to the Don," so really to me, I just saw it as Smiley going through a slight hiccup that he'd soon overcome, although it was apparent that he was spending a lot of time with his own thoughts. I could tell by the tone in his voice that he'd give anything to turn the clock back and be that young Smiley Culture, sprinting against Jubert on the Wandsworth Road.

One day I told him that I was coming over to see him and he said okay, but then before I could leave he rang me back and said he'd visit me instead. When he arrived he was with Donovan, who was driving him. He told me the reason why he'd stopped me from going to him was because he wouldn't have been able to let me leave. He was longing for the kind of company that would ease some of the tension. He said he was in total shock and despair to know that the police could freeze all his assets without finding him with any illegal substance.

He said that he couldn't pay his bills, that his money was frozen; he had no means of travel and couldn't even afford a haircut. I gave him all the encouragement that I could, but things were different now. I'd set up Code 7 by then, and it had started to flourish. I was now mentoring the next generation of disenfranchised young people – my workload had become demanding, and many youngsters and other people were relying on me. One thing that always comes to mind about Smiley is that he had unbelievable front. He would front any situation against all odds and usually come out okay. That's what he had in abundance – front. He would make you believe that he had backing from people in a place where he was a total stranger, or even that he had a gun on him when it was nothing of the sort. Yet Smiley was also someone who would scream at a spider in the house and beg someone to kill it. He once jumped up on the settee at the house in Streatham screaming when a tiny mouse ran in from the garden, and he was that same friend of mine who pulled me in front of him when the yardie kicked the rat in our studio in New Cross, and left me traumatised. Still, Smiley was always there for me in times of need, no matter the situation.

Little things like when I dropped my car keys in a drain in Harlesden and called him to pick up my spare keys from my mum's house - he did it immediately, even though he was way across the other side of London on business. He helped me out after some bad man had mistaken me for Mikey Militant back in the day, and when a dirty scoundrel sneakily robbed my two gold bracelets in Brixton, Smiley was first on the scene to support me. Even when our bond wasn't so close anymore he was still someone I could turn to. When my car was clamped outside my house and I didn't have the £800 the company was demanding he came straight over, gave me £1,000 and said "deal wid it Seny". From the first time we met, Smiley showed a respect for me that was unmatchable. I witnessed how some DJs gained success and disregarded the partners they grew up or jammed with. But in that respect, Smiley was different as he kept me close when the real star time came his way. He was blessed with a mindset that craved for bigger and greater things and he tried to imbue me with that same mentality.

Personally, I accepted Smiley for who he was and didn't expect anything from him apart from friendship. It also went without saying that I would be there for him too.

Twice I stood as a witness for him in court, and helped him overcome difficult criminal cases that were filed against him. One time the prosecutor went as far to suggest that we'd conferred to manipulate the evidence. When this prosecutor realised that I wasn't replying, he reiterated what he'd said so I replied, 'I thought I was here to answer questions, not suggestions'. Everyone in the court found it funny. Even the judge thought he'd repeat my rhyme, "Yes he is here to answer questions, and not suggestions". The point I'm making is that Smiley and I went to great lengths to ensure we had each other's back, and that same sentiment was true of all our clique. Everyone played their part in keeping the unit together. Smiley helped every one of us, and every one of us helped him in return. Mikey, Fox, Peter King and Madla all believed in our brother Smiley and displayed loyalty at its finest. I recall Madla, our exuberant and comical friend, helping Smiley when a girl filed a charge against him. He went to her house and pleaded with both the girl and her sister to drop the charge. Madla's natural persistence finally broke their resistance and fortunately for Smiley, they agreed to drop the charge.

When a girl who'd Smiley had met in a rave the night before stole his big gold chain from his house in Streatham, it was Madla who took him to north London to search for her. They had no clue at all where she lived, apart from she lived in north London, but Madla's expert knowledge of people and places ensured that they found her. It was a reminder of how it's good to have people around you who can find things.

What all this meant now was that I was ready to support my brethren Smiley again in his time of need. It didn't matter that he was down and didn't have any money, because we'd started out with no money. It wasn't the fact that he was Smiley Culture either, because he'd always been Smiley Culture and that had never changed. The fact is that he was the best and kindest friend I ever had and will probably ever have. My heart is still aching and I can feel the lump in my throat as I prepare to reconstruct events of his death from my perspective.

On Monday March 14th 2011, Smiley called to ask me if I could provide a character reference that I'd promised him. After telling him 'yes,' he said that he'd come to see me at my flat in Brixton the following morning.

His mood was certainly more upbeat and the way he was talking about the case showed that he had a lot more optimism about getting through it. I waited two hours for him but eventually had to leave the flat. He called me again and said he was outside the flat but I apologised and told him that I'd had to move, but we could talk later. I then missed a call from him as I was in a meeting and decided I wouldn't ring him back that night, but would call him in the morning to arrange a time for me to go with him to his solicitors. On the morning of Tuesday March 15th, I put on a suit to represent my brethren Smiley and rang him, but his mobile went straight to voicemail. I immediately had the feeling that something wasn't right because Smiley's phone was always on. Maybe his battery was down or he'd had a very late night, but deep down it still felt strange. By around 10 am I received a phone call from someone asking me if Smiley was okay. When I finished that call, another one came through from Barry Boom, and then another from someone else, with everyone asking the same thing. I quickly phoned Donovan and he told me that his dad had passed. It still never sank in and so I instinctively got in my car and drove to Smiley's house. On the way my mobile phone was popping off, the news was spreading so fast.

As I reached his house in Warlingham I was on the phone to Mannix, and he heard me talking to the officer outside Smiley's house. There was a marked police car parked on the outside of Smiley's drive, but the front gates of his house were shut. The police car was facing towards the road and I noticed there were officers inside the car. I got out of my car, approached the police vehicle and asked them if I could see my friend. The police asked me to move away from the house, and told me that they'd speak to me in a minute. Soon afterwards a policeman approached me and said that there was nothing he could say. I asked if Smiley was okay and he repeated that he could say nothing. I asked why he was being so cagey but his whole aura was unappealing and his mannerism was blunt, which led me to leave the scene with my head in a spin. On arriving back in Brixton I rang Donovan again and asked him what was going on. This time when he told me it sunk in, the tears flooded my face and I couldn't even speak properly to him on the phone. I somehow blubbered out that I'd call him later. I had to get home quickly to sit down. My phone was still popping off with calls from people who were in shock, and shouting and screaming that the police had killed Smiley.

I rang my daughter who was out in the West End with her friends, shopping and celebrating her 17th birthday. I broke the news to her and although we tried to hold it together, we both broke down in tears as we were saying goodbye. Madla called and we cried on the phone, then he checked me the next day and we cried again as we hugged each other. I received calls from London, all over England and even some from overseas as the news continued to spread like wildfire. Ricky Rainbow called from Chicago, crying in a state and Mike Chicago was crying uncontrollably as well. Fox had tears in his eyes and was trying to be a man about it whilst Mikey kept saying over and over that he just couldn't believe it. Meanwhile, Stewie Love was so emotional that he couldn't even speak.

Maxi Priest called me up in a state of shock and then after the news had sank in, he rang me back later that night screaming how, "they killed him, they killed him..."

My mind was in confusion and although everyone around me strongly believed that the police had killed Smiley, I still had his suicide threats ringing in my head. Up until this day, I am still confused about what happened on that ill-fated morning of March 15th.

This date has now become my 9/11 because why didn't the police handcuff him right away? How could he pull a knife from an UNKNOWN location? Why did the police handcuff him when as they say, he had a knife embedded in his chest? And what were the police really doing during the time they spent in the house? If the history regarding this type of altercation between the police and African-Caribbean community is anything to go by, then I'm afraid we will never get the answer to these questions.

Even if we do get any hint of truth about what really happened to him it will probably be in about twenty years' time, after some ex-police officers decide to come clean in the hope of repenting their sins. It was the people who knew and loved him that made this miserable period at least a little more bearable for me as they turned up in droves to voice their disapproval of the circumstances surrounding his death, whilst simultaneously showing their respect for a true UK DJ legend.

Hundreds of people attended a public meeting held at the Karibu Centre in Brixton the day after Smiley's passing, and a next one held at Lambeth Town Hall attracted thousands more as the overflow of people stretched outside onto the road.

Lee Jasper, a cultural advisor to former London Mayor Ken Livingstone, acted as chairman. He spoke about the need for a change of policies regarding the policing of African-Caribbean people, whilst Merlin headed the Smiley Culture Campaign, and addressed the amount of deaths in police custody.

As someone who most people identified as being close to Smiley both professionally and personally, I focused on his many achievements before reciting something that I'd written for him called 'Character Reference.'

I'd only just finished writing these lyrics as a tribute for Smiley and they were nowhere near ready for me to chat. My emotions were still unsteady and my entire body felt like a ship struggling on rough seas. Attempting to chat lyrics that were so raw and heartfelt was daunting to say the least, but then almost without me being aware of it, the mic was placed in my hand and so I took a deep breath, and prepared to address the mass of people packed in the Town Hall.

"Smiley is loved by every nation,
From English down to all European,
Jamaican and all-round the Caribbean.

Ghanaian, Nigerian and all African.

Smiley start pon a sound by the name Buchanan.

Lansdowne in Stockwell, just behind the station.

And him start to get him lyrical reputation

Wid lyrics like, "Me can't tek me damn tailor."

Him chat nuff sound all over Brixton.

Coxsone, Front Line, Stereograph, Studio 1.

King Tubby's, Supertone, too much fi mention.

One lyrics Smiley tek and ram the session.

"Cain and Abel sat around the table.

Cain say to Abel, 'beg you pass me an apple?'

When I was a youth I used to read up my bible.

Now me tu'n a man, me just turn Jah disciple..."

I hesitated on the next line as my mind was caught up in other thoughts, and I didn't know the lyrics fully. The crowd of people didn't care though. They yelled in appreciation, and urged me to continue with the lyrics.

"Next was Saxon in Lewisham.

Me say Peter King come ask him if him thief him song.

Him say, "which song dat?" King say, "The fast style man."

Smiley laugh and den him write 'Slam Bam.'

"Slam bam, Jah man say hear dem fashion.

Me strong, me long, me at the mic stand.

Say in mi ring, mi wear mi diamond..."

Smiley help Saxon to tu'n a champion.

And him come up wid the hit, 'Cockney Translation.'

Dennis Rowe said, "I told him to write that one."

Anyway in the reggae charts it go No. 1."

Every time I got to Smiley's songs, the crowd sang along with the lyrics and gave rapturous applause. I was overwhelmed with it all. I had mixed feelings of satisfaction and discontent, and struggled to maintain composure as I returned to my seat. On one important level, the entire atmosphere felt uneasy and stank of injustice. The people wanted a message they could hold onto, and some kind of signal that their support was needed. Ultimately, they wanted a plan of action they could follow.

Word of the date, time and venue of the Nine Night travelled fast – almost as fast as a Smiley and Asher combination, so it was destined to be ram-packed and rocking.

Nine Nights And A Funeral

In Ireland they have a wake after someone's died, and in certain parts of Eastern Europe a person's death is celebrated forty days after their passing. In our community we share condolences and memories while singing hymns and eating food together. Our Nine Nights resemble parties much more than they resemble wakes. The Music Bar in Brixton Hill was the venue chosen for Smiley's Nine Night and the owner, C. K Flash provided the night for free without any hesitation. His friendship with Smiley was built on respect so he was more than happy to give support. From the minute he opened the doors at 7 pm on March 24th until he closed them at 5.30 am, his Music Bar was full of people.

I arrived at the Nine Night in a reserved mood. I was definitely not thinking of chatting on the mic and just intended to drink as much champagne as I could to help alleviate the burden I was carrying. I was still outside the Music Bar conversing with friends and fans when someone emerged from the venue stating that people were looking for me inside. He brought our attention to the action that was taking place on the mic and said Tippa Irie was mashing it up.

I made my way inside and was literally mobbed by people giving their condolences, while at the same time urging me to go on the mic. As I entered the actual dancehall where the miniature stage was situated I felt my heart skip a beat as I made my way closer to the performers. Could I really perform in the fragmented state of mind I was in? Tippa was reeling off lyrics as if he was back in the 1980s and as I stood next to him, all my reservations disappeared, and the old-time DJ spirit possessed me. I no longer felt threatened by the fact that I hadn't DJed for a considerable amount of time, and reached for the mic from Tippa. "Yo people, respect high like a mountain and flow like a fountain. Big up Smiley Culture, we love you..." I zoned in on the many artists and celebrities that were present and decided to introduce them one by one so they could give their tributes to Smiley. Tippa Irie, Maxi Priest, Daddy Colonel, Lorna G, Stewie Love, Ragga G, Willie Major, Marshall Lee, Carolene Thompson, Poppy, Tony Williams, Commander B, Beres Bassa, Paul Culture, Madla and more blessed the evening. The people who were there enjoyed the entertainment immensely, and when we'd finished chatting on the mic they craved more. You can see clips of Smiley's Nine Night on YouTube, so thumbs up as usual.

While I chilled outside the venue, wishing people safe journeys, I could feel a sadness lurking amidst the general air of celebration. As the people left, every one of them asked to be notified of the funeral and any other associated event. It was Smiley's sister Laura who put aside her despair and sorrow to organise the funeral. She was Smiley's only sister and the relationship they had was one of pure family love. In the early years we saw a lot of her but as time went by I mainly saw her at family occasions. Smiley always spoke about her so I knew their connection was still tight, and whenever she saw me she greeted me as her brother.

Laura's gentle and courteous demeanour disguised the real depth of her confidence and straightforwardness. It wouldn't take too long for anyone to realise that she never mixed her words. She obviously knew the level of public interest Smiley's funeral would generate and while taking all aspects into account, she decided that it would be more feasible and hold more value if it were a small funeral for family and close friends. Her mother's sanity and welfare were her main concerns, and all else was just procedure that she knew had to be done. Laura became a general and foot soldier all in one.

She planned the event as if she was preparing for war and acted on her own orders as if she was defending her country. Laura was fixated on giving her brother a perfect family send off and insisted that it was about David Emmanuel, and not Smiley Culture. People were pissed, but deep down they knew she had a point. How else would the family have been able to pay their proper respects? All the family yearned for was to be able to embrace his memory and celebrate his life together, as a family. In total, around 250 guests attended the funeral, even though only 150 were invited. It took place in southeast London and was a special, but emotional day. People were elegantly dressed, and graced the proceedings beautifully. It was peacefully quiet outside Laura's house while we waited for the hearse to arrive, but as I stood innocently questioning myself about the reality of the day, a piercing, high-pitched scream snapped me out of my thoughts and alerted me to the hearse's arrival. Smiley's daughter Natara held her stomach as she gasped for more air to summon another scream. I didn't know what to do, much less say, and couldn't even speak for fear of losing my composure and bawling at a level that even Natara's scream would have found hard to match.

I was relieved to see family members consoling Natara and hurried to my car, where I paused for a moment in meditation.

Was all of this really happening? As I meditated, lyrics from my track 'To Who Respect Is Due' kept coming into my head...

"Smiley Culture, respect is due to me and you.
And when we dead the government fi build a statue,
'Ca to who respect is due, respect it must go through..."

The lyrics kept replaying in my mind until a family member knocked on my window and invited me to travel in one of the procession cars. As I sat in the limousine next to Smiley's brothers Rocky and Butch, and also Laura and their mum, reality kicked in and I struggled to keep my emotions intact. The drive was long and it seemed like an age before we got to the church, although I must admit Rocky kept it interesting with his non-stop bad boy chatter that had the others pleading with him to behave himself. Prior to the funeral I had taken on the responsibility of all the music arrangements so my main intention was to ensure that the equipment was set up right, and the band was ready. My friend the singer and dancer Teejah arranged the choir, and Maxi Priest rehearsed them alongside the musicians.

It was a special treat for me to work with Maxi after so many years and it eased some of the tension during the build-up. Maxi was sincere in his desire to create a ballad in tribute to Smiley and I was amazed at the expertise and professionalism that he'd developed over the years. Stewie Love and Mannix were charged with singing the song 'My Friend' at the church, but I'd always intended to call up Maxi and ask him to sing along with them once the song started. After a while our eyes "made four" as I gestured towards him, and he walked onto the stage to stretch his vocal cords. It was now nearly time for me to read the eulogy. That was okay by me, since I knew that I only had to make sure my emotions didn't get the better of me while I was reading. However, the decision to display slides of Smiley and his memorabilia right before my appearance made it even more difficult than I'd realised. I had to look to the floor and blot out all else whilst sat there, trying to stay focused on what I was going to say. Finally, it was time. I kissed Smiley's mum on the cheek and made my way to the stage. It was a nice surprise to see Donovan join me as he took his position on my left. I acknowledged Militant Mikey as he stood to my right and began with my introduction. "Where's my reading glasses man? Cha'..."

That broke the ice and I was away. I tore into the eulogy as if I were on stage performing hot lyrics for the TV cameras. I asked people to stand and show themselves when I mentioned their names in the eulogy and paused in a section of it as I gave credit to Smiley's mum. I reminded her of how much Smiley had loved her and thanked her sincerely for being like a mum to me as well.

The choir was something else. When I got to the part in the eulogy where I sang a few songs that Smiley liked, they harmonised so well that anyone would have thought we'd rehearsed it. They truly brought tidings of comfort and joy to the occasion. I finished the reading on a positive note and whilst turning to thank Donovan, was taken aback at hearing the standing ovation I received. I was surprised, but at the same time grateful for such a dancehall style appreciation of my first-ever public reading. Whilst extending my gratitude to the people, I couldn't help but hope that Smiley was watching from his spiritual home, chilling on his throne with his feet up, tuned in with a big fat spliff in his hand and proclaiming, "That's my Seny!"

Throughout the rest of the funeral my thoughts were firmly fixated on the fact that I would never be able to confer with Smiley in his physical form again. I looked at his name in my phone's contact list several times, and couldn't yet accept the reality that I wouldn't see his name being displayed anymore when my phone rang. There was going to be a massive gap in my life and I had no desire to fill it. As the burial took place, the downbeat mood of the people forced me to seek my own silent sanctuary. Not even five minutes passed before someone found me chilling in another part of the cemetery, and came to let me know that my presence was again required at the graveside. The people wanted something to alleviate the doom and gloom – something that injected the feeling of life back into proceedings. Something creative and imaginative that would help them dispel the sadness and give them positive memories of Smiley Culture that they could embrace in harmony. I asked Smiley's mum if she minded if I performed a tribute to her son and she replied, "Big up Smiley Culture". That was all the encouragement I needed and while I stood by the open graveside, surrounded by beautiful flowers, I chatted 'Character Reference' in acapella style.

One of my protégés called Face, who'd graduated through the ranks of my charity Code 7, remained at my side from the day we heard the news about Smiley's passing and was committed to helping in any way that he could. Being an artist himself, Face learned 'Character Reference' from start to finish. He took great pleasure in performing the backing vocals and stood proudly by my side, giving me that extra portion of encouragement that I needed and welcomed. It was an honourable day, a day of mourning and yet still a day of celebration for Smiley Culture's life. To a few of my long-term friends it was a day that brought home the unpredictability of life and the significance of real friendship. Fox ushered me, Militant Mikey, Stewie Love and Mannix to one side and reminded us that the last time we'd seen each other was at another funeral, and asked if we were going to wait for another funeral before we saw each other again. It was a point well made, and well taken. We agreed to meet up weekly as "old-school" man dem so we could bring back regularity to our friendship, and we've done so ever since. Smiley's funeral had opened our eyes and we were now seeing clearly. It's at these weekly meetings where we speak about old times, current affairs and future plans.

Smiley is often on the agenda which is duly warranted, since the meetings were originally formed in his honour. It doesn't matter if we watch a movie or a football game, play some tunes or simply sit there and don't speak. The fact is that we meet weekly, and it's the one meeting that I look forward to most out of my busy agenda. These meetings have also helped to bring added purpose to our lives as we've already promoted raves, arranged empowerment seminars and contributed in various ways towards helping others. Sometimes, as bizarre as it may seem, we've all admitted to feeling Smiley's presence with us in certain meetings. Many times someone would say something and the others would say, "Raaa, you sounded just like Smiley" or "that's something Smiley would have said". Behind closed doors Smiley Culture's name lives on, while people have openly continued to show their support by attending inquiries, hearings and most notably the Justice For Smiley Culture march. They came in their thousands, carrying banners and placards and crying out for justice as they marched from the Wandsworth Road through Parliament Square to Scotland Yard, remonstrating in an orderly and peaceful fashion whilst campaigning to make their voices heard.

Walking behind a float, kicking reggae beats through the streets of Westminster, thousands marched on April 16th 2011 to demand justice for the vaguely explained death of Smiley Culture and the many other people who'd also died in police custody. When the marchers reached Scotland Yard, Merlin and Lee Jasper demonstrated neat balancing skills as they delivered their speeches from high up on a ladder. With the backing of the people, they demanded a public inquiry and vowed to continue protesting until one was confirmed. Once more I focused my attention on highlighting Smiley Culture and his achievements while with help from people below, I balanced on the ladder and chatted the lyrics to 'Character Reference'. I could see the police massed in front of Scotland Yard glaring over in my direction, and it was obvious they were listening keenly to every word that was being said.

My respect, as always, goes out to the people. Their support was a vital factor in helping to diminish and overcome obstacles in the Emmanuel family's campaign for justice. The people were there at the start of Smiley's career, and they were there in the end. I'll never forget the expressions of shock, sorrow and pain on their faces when the news first broke.

Most of them if not all, were fans of Smiley Culture who remembered the 1980s and wanted to reminisce about not just his music, but also that whole era of UK DJ music. Community radio stations played 'Police Officer', 'Mi God Mi King' and 'Abbreviation Qualification' as they readdressed their appreciation of those days, and friends still call me now to tell me that one of mine or Smiley's old tracks are playing on the radio. Sometimes I even hear one or two being played myself, and I stop to listen with renewed interest as I now tour parts of Europe again.

Fans always used to say that we were ahead of our time and we can see the truth of that now. They say that most of our old lyrics still carry the same weight, and there are so many new DJs reinventing our topics, styles and lyrics that I struggle to know where to begin. One thing's for sure – DJs are still impersonating Smiley's habit of switching accents, and especially when they're referring to the police in their lyrics. He made an everlasting impression on so many people, both with his lyrics and character, but none more so than on me. He was the first to tell people that I inspired him but despite the fact that he's now departed, he's still a strong inspiration for me.

His go-get attitude, never-say-die willpower and "money have fi spend" mentality will never desert me as I continue on my journey. I miss the phone calls where we used to speak to each other at least seven times a day and I miss the gatherings at his plush house where we reminisced about old times, but most of all I miss the man himself. He's still the first person that comes into my head when I want to share a special brethren moment with someone close, and his is still the first name in my head whenever I think back on my music career. The final time that we raved together at the Victoria Hotel back in 2011 was the last personal test of our friendship. Smiley had £5,000 in his pouch that night and bought a bottle of champagne for each member of our eight-man posse. It was standard Smiley Culture raving procedure – a corner captured, champagne popping and bling gleaming as we rocked to the pumping music. All eyes were on us and Smiley was in his usual high spirits, leading the posse from the front and bussing some rude boy dance moves, when he stopped abruptly and appeared to be looking for something. His 22 carat, white gold diamond ring had flown off his finger in the middle of one of his over-elaborate dance routines, and slid somewhere into the darkness of the dancehall.

His facial expression said it all, because he wasn't happy. In fact he was pissed, and said that if he didn't find it he would ask the soundmen to stop the music and turn on the lights. I really don't know why, but I walked to the other side of the dancehall, looked down on the floor and spotted something shiny. I apologised to the two guys who were standing there and quickly reached down to pick up the object. It felt very heavy for something so small, and so I knew that it was Smiley's ring even before I looked at it. As I made my way back over to him I couldn't help but imagine how much the ring was worth and what the odds were on me actually finding it. I handed it to him and uttered the words, 'It looks like I was meant to find it and give it to you'. That small show of friendship obviously ran deep in Smiley's mind because after the rave he rang me early in the morning for some idle chitchat. I think it perhaps took his mind back to the days when we rolled together, and kicked it like karate every day, experiencing each other's loyalty regularly. I know that I will never have such a friendship again but as I've said, I still have the memories. I have some old Buchanan and in-house cassettes that we recorded with Smiley jamming on them and they keep his memory alive within me.

Every time I listen to them I remember something else he said or something we did. So long live Smiley Culture's name, and God bless his soul.

Pictures From Funeral

ɔm left: Fox, Asher Senator, Paul Culture, Maxi Priest, Militant Mikey, Face

Asher with Sam, GJ and another of Smiley's old mates at funeral

Culture's resting place

Smiley's school friend Clint, his nephew Merlin, good friend
Lloydie, Face, his school friend Dennis and good friend Carolene

Pictures From The March

Asher Senator performing 'Character Reference'

Serious turn out

Character Reference

For DAVID EMMANUEL also known as "SMILEY CULTURE".

Written by Asher Senator on 30. 03. 2011.

Victor David Emmanuel, also known to many as Smiley Culture, was born on February 10th 1963 to Cyril and Gwendaline Emmanuel. His parents were Guyanese immigrants who came to this country in the early 60's and settled in the area of South West London. David was the last of five siblings, comprising of three brothers, Desmond, Cyril, Richard and sister Laura. He was blessed with four children - a son Donovan, daughters Natara and Shanice and one adopted son Tai.

David went to Santley Primary School, Brixton and attended secondary school at Tulse Hill Boy's School. His favourite subjects were Electronics, English, Economics and Maths. He had a keen eye for business and was an entrepreneur from a very young age.

David loved watching martial arts movies and amassed quite a collection of various movies on both Betamax and VHS formats. Sports-wise, he loved table tennis, and used to take his nephews Justin and Stephen to play table tennis as young boys in Ferndale Sports Centre in Brixton. David had his own bat, and to all intents and purposes took the sport seriously. While in secondary school, he earned the name "Smiley" from his infectious personality and skill in influencing others. He used to lay bets with his male school friends about the odds of him being able to make a girl stranger smile while she was passing by. Smiley said he used to approach the girl-strangers and say to them, "Please smile for me and I will give you some money out of a bet I just made". He said it always worked. They smiled, he collected his winnings and then later he would find the girls and give them a cut of his earnings.

In 1977, whilst living in Lansdowne Green Estate, Smiley began to chat on a sound-system by the name of Buchanan, and whilst the trend was to imitate the lyrics from Jamaican dancehall tapes in those days, Smiley made sure that he mainly copied cultural lyrics, hence the name "Culture" – Smiley Culture.

Character Reference

It was during our time on Buchanan that Smiley and I became close friends, mainly because of our lyrical compatibility and the similarities in what we liked. We became even closer when one day, while driving my first car, we had an accident on Ferndale Road. My car was full of friends, but when it was clear that the car couldn't be driven any further, everyone said goodbye and left Smiley and I to it. He stayed with me and made sure that we sorted the car out.

In the early '80s, music and lyrics were Smiley's first love but making money was his motivation. He tried different trades and hustles like selling insurance, buying and selling watches and cars and giving out loans with interest on repayments.

His first car was a Fiat. He then bought his Lancia and he even bought an orange Audi which we said looked like a BMW so to us, it *was* a BMW. Smiley also liked to challenge people who thought they were fast runners to a sprint race. Believe me he made money from that too. And when Smiley realised that I could do one-arm press-ups, believe me, he made money from that too!

Yes, he made money from a variety of ways but at the end of the day, music and lyrics kept him contented and focused within himself. Most of the time, Smiley would be amongst close friends and doing music. The original team was Smiley, Asher, Willie Major and Vico D, but then Willie Major and Vico D left the team and so Militant Mikey and Fox became a significant part of what was happening and what was to become. We were together most of the time, hence the arguments with our girlfriends about how, "you're always with Smiley".

When the lyrics business started to expand and original lyrics became the highlight for the people, Smiley started to write lyrics that when we look back on them now, were certainly ahead of their time. During the early '80s, he was writing lyrics like 'Me Cant Tek Me Damn Tailor' – a lyrical reference to his tailor who cut one sleeve longer than the other. He wrote lyrics like 'Tell Me What You Want For Your Birthday' and 'Tell Me What You Want For Your Wedding' – two lyrics that certainly had the potential to be year-on-year dancehall smashes.

He also wrote the legendary 'Cain and Abel' – a lyrical rhyme that started and ended with the syllable "ble" over the equivalent of three records.

He performed his lyrics on almost every local sound-system around town. We're talking about Sir Coxsone, Front Line, Stereograph, Studio One, King Tubby's, Supertone, Black Harmony, Small Axe, Soprano B, Taurus and more. Smiley Culture apprentices started to spring up all over town such as Paul Culture and Joe 90, to name just two.

This was great fun as Smiley mashed up dance after dance, but there was a problem. No money was being made from music; he was doing it entirely for the love of it. By 1982, a friend called Everton Skully asked Smiley and I to perform at a club in North London called the Four Aces. Smiley and I performed one lyrics apiece, we did quite well and when we finished, Skully paid us £5 each. £5 each, and yet Smiley and I celebrated so much. We had been paid for our lyrics at last!

Character Reference

On April 15th 1983, Smiley was offered the chance to perform on his first official stage show. This was at the Riverdale Centre in Lewisham and was promoted by his long-term friend Dennis Rowe from Saxon and singer Maxi Priest, who would also become Smiley's good friend. This was all fine but it just so happened that the previous week in Brixton at the Aces Club (which is now The Fridge), Smiley and I encountered an awkward night after we'd agreed to chat for Saxon because their DJs hadn't turn up.

We were two Brixton DJs chatting in Brixton on a sound from Lewisham and the club was so quiet you could hear a pin drop. This affected Smiley and I so much that we sat in the car outside of his flat in Union Grove for four hours, speaking about the embarrassment and "how we do not need this", "how we don't have to take this from people" and "how we may as well give up and just make money". In the end, Smiley and I decided to give the Riverdale Centre event a go and said if we did not do well there, then we would certainly give up the DJ thing for good. Five minutes before we were due to appear on stage, Smiley and I stood to the side and we prayed to God to let us do well that night.

Obviously, God truly answered. After this event, Smiley became a Saxon DJ, performing his lyrics at dances across London. Sometimes in the daytime we would visit Dennis Rowe and Muscle Head of Saxon at their homes, and it was on one of those visits when Dennis Rowe inspired Smiley to write 'Cockney Translation'.

The early '80s saw the rise of controversial traffic warden schemes and when I wrote 'Traffic Warden Don't Give Me No Ticket' Smiley said he was inspired to write 'Police Officer,' as the police were always a thorn in our sides. In 1984, after Papa Levi released his hit song 'Mi God Mi King', the talk about Smiley recording music started coming fast and furious as different music producers started to approach him. He was eventually offered a contract by Chris Lane and John McGillivray, who were the proprietors of Fashion Records in Clapham Junction. Smiley and I sat down and he spoke to me about his fears of recording the track that Fashion wanted, which was 'Cockney Translation'. He was concerned about how the black public would receive him when he did the cockney accent. I remember reminding him of the tremendous response that these lyrics were already receiving in dancehalls.

He said, "You sign for this label too Seny, and we can do this". Smiley made sure that I signed for Fashion Records also and as you know, history was created.

'Cockney Translation' went to Number 1 in the UK reggae charts while his biggest hit 'Police Officer' went to No. 12 in the UK national charts, even though at the time it was selling to the equivalent of a No. 1 pop song. After publicist Alan Edwards began managing Smiley's PR, the brand Smiley Culture quickly grew in status. Interviews, articles and a whole range of publicity surrounded Smiley and he made sure that Asher was always there.

Still in the '80s, when Smiley and I began to charge a nice, but small fee for us to perform three songs each at events, Maxi Priest said to us "You can't do that, you're extorting the business". Smiley and I always referred back to this in later years as we used to say, "You see how much Max is charging for shows now – thousands!"

Although times were getting more and more exciting and Smiley's schedule became full, he always found time for his mum and to chill and play the music he loved. Smiley loved songs like 'Mama may have, papa may have – but God bless the child that has his own' by Billie Holiday.

He also loved songs like, 'the more you give to life, is the more you're gonna get from life' by Bob Andy; 'Marcus Garvey words come to pass' by Burning Spear and 'Let Me Down Easy' by Dennis Brown.

Oh yes, believe it or not we still had trouble at certain dance gates where some bouncers did not want to let us in easily, maybe due to jealousy or something. Anyhow, Smiley made sure we always got in. On one occasion, we arrived at the Podium Suite in Vauxhall (which is now the Coliseum) and the gate men refused to allow us entry. Smiley was fuming and began to let them know how upset he was. In contrast, I was reasoning with one of the bouncers saying, "Let us in and we will give you options to work on some of our new up-and-coming shows". Smiley stopped me in my tracks and said, "Don't talk to them nice Seny!"

He bought his first music studio and installed it in his mum's flat in Lansdowne Green Estate.

He met a top studio technician called Tim Owen who helped to wire it up and Smiley would always call on him whenever he needed a studio to be connected. This little biddly studio served its purpose as it was used to record local friends of Smiley who were truly talented. People like Mannix, a singer who because of Smiley, has gone on to make singing his profession. People like Stuart Love, another singer who still smashes raves whenever he sings live. After Fashion Records, Smiley signed for Polydor and was lining up to release his first album. However, due to a dispute amongst the record companies that particular album was delayed. Then in 1985, he was approached by Trevor Philips to audition as host of a new TV show on Channel 4 called Club Mix. Smiley passed the audition with flying colours and Club Mix was broadcasted for two years, reaching over one million viewers on the last series. It featured artists such as Millie Jackson, Tiger and the late Delroy Wilson and Smiley was a favourite of them all.

He also recorded a TV commercial for Nat West Bank; a radio advert for London Transport and thanks to his friend Sam Dundas, made an appearance in the ITV series The Bill.

In the late '80s, he established his first official recording studio in New Cross courtesy of Charlie Richardson and Gypsy Johnny, who loved Smiley and his music. The name of this company was Hap'nin Productions. As the years went by, Smiley signed many artists to Hap'nin, including Glamour Kid, Mark Morrison, Stevie Hoang, the youth band Future, Merlin his nephew and many, many more. However, it was I who was left in charge of the studio in New Cross when Smiley, Mikey and Fox went to America for Smiley to record an album with Run DMC.

Smiley bought his first house in Streatham and when the lease for the studio in New Cross expired, he set up the studio there instead. It was in this studio where he recorded a track with former world heavyweight boxing champion Lennox Lewis.

Smiley asked Fox and Mikey to write the lyrics for Lennox, "I'm on a mission – to seek and destroy"... How well did Lennox rap on the track? Well, let's just say that Lennox is a great boxer!

Character Reference

Using his music royalties, Smiley started to take friends, colleagues and music people on flights around Europe and eventually around the world. At times he would even pay for up to ten people or more to travel with him. On one occasion he took eleven people to MIDEM, the annual music conference in France. In 1989, Smiley linked up with Danny Sims, the original manager of Bob Marley, and launched the record label WAM in Edgware Road. This is where he met and worked with greats from America like Jocelyn Brown and Oliver Cheatham, and formed close friendships with singer Ricky Rainbow and producer Michael Barnes from Chicago. It was around this time that Smiley signed a record deal with SBK from America for the same album that he'd recorded and since regained from Polydor.

After a year or so, when SBK prolonged the release of the album, Smiley reclaimed it from then and signed it to Virgin Records. When Virgin then also delayed its release, Smiley reclaimed the album yet again.

From the '90s and right into the 2000s, Smiley was helping people to get jobs within the music industry.

Character Reference

People like Mickey D who was at Warner Brothers and Darcus who is now at Universal. All the key personnel at the major record companies knew Smiley and some even felt intimidated by him. For example when Warner Brothers were taking forever to pay Smiley on one of his contracts, he said to me, "Asher, Christmas is coming", then went there and ensured that they wrote and signed his outstanding cheque immediately.

One person of great significance that Smiley met was the Queen. He met her at the Commonwealth Institute and everyone removed their hats except for Smiley. The Queen even made reference to his beaver by saying, "I do like your hat!"

After he opened a music production house in Harlesden that he'd kitted out nicely this was of great benefit to all of us including myself, Smiley's nephew Mark, his son Donovan and Madla, who was a strong part of the team. Smiley moved to Croydon and again set up a studio where he recorded a variety of artists like Ricky Rainbow and Paul Robinson, aka Barry Boom. He later moved to Warlingham, which would prove his last place of residence.

Character Reference

He formed close friendships with Orville and Courtney who were always there for him, Dignitary Jim Brathwaite, Roger Diamond, Gammo Speng, Jessus from Coxsone, Commander B, Mark Smart, Junior Speng and others. He had a tight relationship with his daughter Natara and was building bonds with his other daughter Shanice and cousin Claudia.

Smiley met many people from a wide range of cultures and trades. He was captivated by the wealth Africa held and at the same time concerned about how some were reaping from it.

He learned about diamonds, gold and other commodities that Africa is blessed with. Smiley learned well and even acquired his own mine. He insisted that it was just a matter of time before he could fulfil his lifelong dream of helping the truly deprived Africans around the world. Most recently, Smiley had a major music contract with a company in Azerbaijan; he was in the process of arranging a tour in China for Lady Gaga and was even preparing to re-launch Smiley Culture the artist.

Son, Brother, Father, Grandfather, Cousin, Uncle and Friend Smiley was articulate, intelligent, caring and very amusing, and he always achieved in whatever he set out to do.

He rode the ups and downs of life and his downs were down but when he was up, there was no one who could match his vibrant personality and enriching spiritual energy. Smiley will be truly missed by those who really knew and loved him, and although he left before his time we know ultimately, that God has taken his beloved son.

WE WILL ALWAYS LOVE YOU DAVID EMMANUEL, SMILEY CULTURE AND MAY YOUR SOUL REST IN PERFECT PEACE.

Buchanan Sound-System

"Juks" Junior was the owner of the sound and the one person trusted by all our parents. My mum often said no until Junior asked. Victor Paisley or "Vico" was one of our most talented mic chanters, alongside Carlton Williams AKA "Dirty Willy" who eventually became "Willy Major." Sweeney was one of the trendier guys in the area, and a proper geezer. He was always making money and looking good, and we called Tony Darnley "Mr. Now you see him now you don't" because of his unorthodox lifestyle. Ron The Builder had an important role, since he was the guy who built and repaired our amplifiers and pre-amps. Big G, bless his soul, will be more familiar as former British Heavyweight Boxing Champion Gary Mason. He had to wear short trousers to secondary school, which was reason enough for us to tease him.

Derek Fenty was Big G's best friend, and a radical loyalist when it came to Buchanan. His brother Kenroy was my best friend when I first moved to Lansdowne Green Estate as a 12 year old.

Winston Jordan was the real joker in the pack although he once squeezed a neighbourhood bully so tightly, the man had to plead for his life. Buchanan certainly didn't lack for muscle. Martin Kettle was nicknamed "Cannon" somewhat after the sound, but mainly because his hands hit like a cannon. Kenny Weir and David Isaacs, or "Natty" as we called him never dodged anything. Those two would always be fighting, whether it was inside, outside or even nowhere near our dances. All we used to hear was people shouting, 'Kenny's fighting,' or 'Natty's fighting someone...' Satchmo and Pedro were two more brothers, and warriors who were happy for any form of trouble that came their way.

Pat Vassell was arrested with a gun just once but the name "Gunman" followed him around for a long time, and poor Simon Elliot got stuck with "Half Caste The Murderer." It's funny, but I can't actually recall or even understand why we would call such a nice person "The Murderer."

The rest of the posse included Lisa Azaar (bless her soul), Beverley Spencer (bless her soul), Marfier Greaves (my son Christopher's mother), Marcia Russell (the mother of Smiley's daughter Natara), Aunt Silvy, Jackie Sharpe (mother of Smiley's son Donovan), Donna Sharpe (mother of my son Darren), Yvonne Sharpe, Valerie Sharpe ("Titch"), Joyce, Marvine Harewood, Gary Taste, Peter Marshall, Fox's sisters Donna and Pat, Joystix, Jackie Pullock, Sharon Pillock ("Buzby"), Mervin, Lucia, Grace, Michael Ellis, Jimmy Bish, Fingers, Bigger, Teddy, Iscent, Donna Darnley, Paul Johnson, Carlton Warren and Whistle G.

Then came the youngsters who built Buchanan No. 2.

Fred Fenty, Stuart Lisbie (Stewie Love), Ricky Vassell, Paul Vassell (who was known as "Paul Culture" after becoming one of Smiley's apprentices), Paul Cumberbatch, Tony Irie, Culture Mark, Leroy Williams (bless his soul), Karl Matthews, Jerry and twins Peter and Paul, Poppy, Danny Johnson ("Danny Dazzler"), Jubert, Christine ("Dolly"), Simon (bless his soul), Jesse Vassell, Sherlock, his sister Marva and Michael Henry.

Terminologies

An interpretation of slang and street wording

Blues Dance/Dance - A rave kept in a flat or house featuring various sound systems that usually went on until the late hours of the morning or even into the next afternoon.

Bredrin – A good friend.

Buss – Having a hit song or becoming very popular. It also means to deliver – i.e., "the crowd want you to BUSS your lyrics" or "What lyrics did you BUSS last night?"

Continuous Rhyming – Lyrics that rhyme all the way through a song, maintaining the same rhyme but with different words that match at the end of each lyrical line.

Dancehall – This term originally referred to the area where dances were kept. It then became the name of an actual music genre – reggae music with higher energy and tempo, now commonly known as "bashment."

Dem – Them

Terminologies

DJ – In our dancehall era, a DJ wasn't someone who played records, but someone who performs his or her lyrics live over the microphone in a dance. Eventually this term was devalued and replaced with the word "MC."

Chat – A term used to describe how we delivered our lyrics – i.e., singers sang their songs and we chat our lyrics.

Chanting – Another, more roots term for "chat."

Dis – Means to disrespect.

Dub Plate or "Special" – An exclusively recorded vocal track by an artist promoting a sound-system and sometimes demoting its rivals. The artist usually converts their own hit lyrics to fit the requirements of the sound-system. Representatives of these sound-systems can pay thousands of pounds for exclusive Dub Plates or Specials.

Forward – Encore.

Line – A lyrical line is the equivalent to 1 bar in music terminology.

Lyrics – Words chatted in a steady flow.

Terminologies

MC - Master of Ceremony, meaning the new and highest level of "DJ."

Mic – Microphone.

PA – Personal Appearance.

Play Out – When a sound system is playing at a dance, event, etc.

Posse – A group of youths who would hang around together, nowadays somewhat loosely referred to as gangs.

Rhyme – Lyrics that match at the end of each line.

Sound-System – A custom-built, super-powered discotheque used to play in clubs, house raves and dance halls, etc.

Sound – Is the shortened term for sound-system.

Steaming – Is when a posse of youths run through a crowd of people snatching handbags, watches and jewellery etc.

Style – The way in which lyrics are melodically delivered.

Balling – Full of money.

Ram – Packed.

Terminologies

Pirating Lyrics – using/chatting other people's lyrics

Dirty Jankrow – Jamaican insult that mainly means 'dirty scavenger/vulture'

Bless his/her soul – Rest in peace

Special Thanks

To the Almighty, Creator of All.

Smiley's mother and family – sister Laura, brothers Butch, Desmond & Rocky, daughter Natara, son Donovan and nephew Merlin. Smiley's school friends Clive, Dennis and Donovan Barnett.

My peeps – Stewie Love, Paul Culture, Militant Mikey, Fox, Coral, Amarah, Chris, Rovena, Darren, Lee-Ann, Sherry, Nicky, Keith Mannix, Madla, Mike Chicago, Jodie, Mike, Face, Code 7 team, Buchanan team, John from Dub Vendor, Chris from Fashion Records, Gussie P, Coxsone team, Front Line team, Saxon team, King Tubby's team and all the sound systems.

Officially - John Masouri for his invaluable editing skills, original proof-reader Sarah Vibes, photographer Aaron Thompson and all who played any part whatsoever in the construction of this book.

Extra Special Thanks to Rickardo Quintyne-Wright for his ingenious help and support in constructing the book and to Peter King for his beautiful painting on the front cover. Thank you and blessings.